**Liberty and Learning**

*Issues and Ideas in Education Series*
edited by Robin Barrow, School of Education,
University of Leicester

Dilemmas of the Curriculum
G. H. BANTOCK

Happiness
ROBIN BARROW

John Stuart Mill's Theory of Education
F. W. GARFORTH

Critical Thinking and Education
JOHN E. McPECK

Educational Practice and Sociology
B. SHAW

Behaviorism and Schooling
IRA STEINBERG

Political Learning in Childhood
OLIVE STEVENS

Fantasy and Common Sense in Education
JOHN WILSON

# Liberty
## and
# Learning

---

**KENNETH A. STRIKE**

*Cornell University*

MARTIN ROBERTSON • OXFORD

First published in 1982 by Martin Robertson & Company Ltd.,
108 Cowley Road, Oxford OX4 1JF.

**British Library Cataloguing in Publication Data**
Strike, Kenneth
  Liberty and Learning. — (Issues and ideas in
  education series)
  1. Education — Philosophy
  2. Liberty
  I. Title   II. Series
  370.1     LA21

  ISBN 0-85520-431-1
  ISBN 0-85520-432-X Pbk

Typeset by Photosetting and Secretarial Services Ltd., Yeovil
Printed and bound in Great Britain by Book Plan Ltd., Worcester.

# Contents

# Preface

Freedom in education was a hot topic a decade ago. Some educators then seemed to me to succumb not only to the need to respect students and their ideas and to be open and intellectually honest, but also to the demand to liberate students from the intellectual heritage represented in the curriculum and from standards of disciplined inquiry and intellectual competence. That many students were, in fact, liberated from such things seems to me to help explain why we are now in reaction against this emphasis on freedom in education.

Since the public pendulum on issues of freedom and authority in education appears to have a fairly short swing, and since the questions are important regardless of whether they are in vogue, it seemed to me to be appropriate to try to take a fresh look at some of the central problems of liberty and learning. I believe the central issue is the nature and extent of the authority we are willing to extend to received ideas. How and when must teachers and students be subservient to an intellectual heritage? Liberal political theory is well attuned to the dangers of giving too much authority to received opinion. We have the examples of the treatment of such as Galileo to remind us that when the state or the church enforce ideas, intellectual progress is retarded. We have not, however, adequately recognized that received ideas must have some kind of authority. If they do not, we lack rational ways to judge new ideas or to make educational decisions. I have thus given considerable energy to working out a view on the authority of ideas.

This has led to an approach that pays a great deal of attention to the theory of knowledge. To the extent that liberty is a handmaiden to inquiry, we need to understand what inquiry is like if we are to understand what liberty should be like. I have looked extensively to the work of Thomas Kuhn, since his views on the growth of knowledge seem to me both roughly correct and to have significant implications for the concepts of liberty and authority in education.

The first part of this book is devoted to trying to understand in abstract philosophical terms how this notion of the authority of received ideas applies to questions of liberty in both educational and civil contexts. The second part is concerned to apply the results of this inquiry to two particular problem areas – academic freedom and student rights. The discussion generates a few loose ends that I try to tie together in rather sketchy fashion in a postscript.

I have generally believed that philosophers are entitled to be a bit more incautious in books than they are in journal articles. The audience is wider and it is often more important to be suggestive and provocative than to be careful and reserved. I have, thus, been willing to be opinionated. As befits a rational agent, I am unsure of much of what I say here and hope to learn from reader reaction. Those readers who are familiar with my earlier work on some of these topics will discover that I at least occasionally change my mind. I will leave it to them to decide if I have learned anything.

I believe this book will be of considerable interest to both the expert and the novice who are seriously concerned with the issues. Reading it will sometimes require intellectual effort. Those who find this problematic, need especially to read it.

Kenneth A. Strike
Cornell University
July 1981

# CHAPTER 1

# The Issues of Liberty and Learning

Should students and teachers be free in educational institutions? Before any answer is attempted, it needs to be pointed out that the question is defective. It asks one to be for or against freedom, and it does this without specifying any clear idea of what one is to be for or against. Surely one cannot answer it in this form.

What seems called for, then, is some way of specifying actions or choices that should be left to the individual's discretion and other actions or choices concerning which the individual may be made responsible to society, the state, the school or some civil authority. Some philosophers, for example, have distinguished between self-regarding and other-regarding acts – those that affect only the person who does them and those that affect the well-being of others. It is usually considered that people are entitled to liberty with respect to self-regarding acts, but they may be held accountable for other-regarding acts. As it is popularly put, people have the right to do whatever they want, as long as they don't harm anyone else.

This strategy has never been highly successful. On examination, the distinction between self-regarding and other-regarding acts is less than clear. Moreover, the strategy is particularly unsatisfactory for examining the role of freedom in education, as it fails to illuminate any obvious connection between any class of educational goals and some particular class of actions that should be free or not free. At least at first blush there is nothing about the doctrine that self-regarding actions should be free that suggests that freedom is a means to some distinctly educational goal. Nor do there seem to be ready to hand

1

arguments of an educational sort that clearly pick out the class of self-regarding acts as those where students are of a right free.

Indeed, the opposite may be the case. There are reasons that suggest that the distinction between self-regarding and other-regarding acts is less than appropriate to illuminate the question of freedom in education. One crucial assumption embedded in the claim that people are entitled to freedom with respect to self-regarding acts is that they are competent to make the choices such liberty entails. But there are reasons why this is systematically unlikely to be the case in educational contexts. Part of the grounds for this claim is that many educational institutions deal with the youngest and thus the most immature part of the population. Children are least likely to possess the competencies prerequisite for autonomy over their own lives. This, however, is not the major consideration. More important is the character of the educational enterprise. Choosing to engage in some educational activity – learning physics, for example – differs significantly from other choices. When one decides to buy a car one normally has a reasonably accurate idea of what a car is and what it is for. Thus, one can make a rational assessment of whether to buy a car and what sort of car to buy. There are difficulties, however, in making such a rational assessment about physics or most other subject matters. One is unlikely to know exactly what physics is unless one has already engaged in the study of it. One can perhaps know some of the benefits contingent on learning physics, and one can have a fuzzy idea of what physics is about. However, to know what physics is, is just that – to know physics. To a large extent, the criteria of evaluation of physics and the values that it realizes are internal to it. Thus, a rational appraisal of the worth of physics is virtually impossible to the uninitiated.

If this argument, which I believe applies to all rational enterprises, is correct, it places significant limits on the extent to which arguments that justify liberty in many areas of conduct can be applied to education. It does not show that freedom has no place in education. Rather, it shows that broad generalizations about the value of liberty should be accepted reluctantly, especially when they concern education. Moreover, it suggests that arguments about liberty that are intended to apply to civil or political contexts should not be generalized to educational contexts uncritically, and it suggests that there may be arguments about liberty that are uniquely educational arguments.

We ought not to forget, however, that educational institutions perform non-educational functions. They serve meals, dispense health care, write parking tickets, and often dispense justice for minor offences. Thus, there may also be arguments, perhaps of a political character, that do not apply to educational situations, but that do apply to educational institutions.

The foregoing observations suggest that a study of liberty and learning might well be devoted to the following two questions:

(1)   What kinds of distinctively educational arguments are there for liberty and what kinds of liberty do they justify?
(2)   How is liberty justified in larger political contexts, and to what extent can these arguments be applied to educational institutions?

These questions set the agenda for this book. In what follows in this introduction I shall sketch some lines of response that will set the stage for later more detailed arguments. Before moving on, however, one more comment on the questions is called for. The distinction between educational and political arguments for liberty has been made because those contexts are in many respects different. We should not, however, lose sight of the fact that political institutions can educate and can be evaluated in terms of their capacity to do so. Nor should we lose sight of the fact that educational institutions have political and social functions. They are, for example, often supposed to promote citizenship or democratic attitudes. We should, then, expect essentially educational arguments to have some application to a broad range of social institutions, and we should expect political goals for education to influence our view of liberty.

Some arguments for liberty see it contributing significantly to some class of educational goals. Here I want to consider several such arguments. My aim in this chapter is not to decide on the adequacy of these arguments, but to get a handle on the kind of arguments they are and thereby to get a firmer grasp on what is relevant to evaluating them.

Consider, then, several rather famous quotations connecting liberty with some educational goal. The first is by Albert Einstein:

> . . . It is in fact nothing short of a miracle that the modern methods of instruction have not yet entirely strangled the holy curiosity of inquiry; for this delicate little plant, aside from stimulation, stands mainly in need of freedom; without this it goes to wrack and ruin without fail.[1]

The second is from John Stuart Mill's essay, 'On Liberty':

> He who lets the world, or his own portion of it, choose his plan of life for him has no need of any other faculty than the ape-like one of imitation. He who chooses his plan for himself employs all his faculties. He must use observation to see, reasoning, and judgment to foresee, activity to gather materials for decision, firmness, and self-control to hold to his deliberate decision. And these qualities he requires and exercises exactly in proportion as the part of his conduct which he determines according to his judgment and feeling is a large one.[2]

The final passage, taken from a statement of senior scholars from South African universities, is quoted with favour by Justice Frankfurter of the US Supreme Court in a case concerning academic freedom:

> . . . A university is characterized by the spirit of free inquiry, its ideal being the ideal of Socrates – 'to follow the argument where it leads.'
> Freedom to reason and freedom for disputation on the basis of observation and experiment are the necessary conditions for the advancement of scientific knowledge. A sense of freedom is also necessary for creative work in the arts which, equally with scientific research, is the concern of the university.[3]

These passages do not say precisely the same thing, but they do at least express a common theme. Einstein sees freedom as a condition of curiosity: how can the desire to find out be nurtured except where one can pursue one's questions where they lead? The desire to know cannot survive where there are forbidden questions or forbidden answers. Mill notes that liberty is a condition of achieving competence for inquiry: people do not acquire abilities for which they have no use. It is, thus, the society in which the individual must rely on his own judgement that will produce people with the competence for sound judgement. Justice Frankfurter appeals to what is often called the market-place of ideas: truth, it is held, is pursued most effectively in an atmosphere where opinions are subjected to the light of open criticism and debate. In various ways, then, liberty is seen as a prerequisite of thought or inquiry. It is the capacity for an effective functioning of thought that is the educational goal to which liberty is a means.

I shall henceforth call arguments of this sort *epistemological arguments*. Epistemology, as I understand it, is concerned to specify the norms of rational inquiry. I understand the phrase 'norms of rational inquiry' as broader than the notion 'rules of valid argument'. Epistemology here is more than logic; it is also concerned with the social and psychological conditions under which rational inquiry can occur.

This conception will be felicitous because the validity of arguments linking liberty and inquiry depends not only on views of a psychological or sociological sort, but also on views of what knowledge is and how it is obtained.

The view that liberty is a means to rational inquiry assumes that knowledge is attainable or at least improvable as the result of human thought. If knowledge, however, depends on authority or if knowledge is impossible, arguments for liberty that see it as a way of protecting the process of inquiry make little sense. To the extent that knowledge is revealed, it is not a function of inquiry. To that extent there is no need to protect the process of inquiry. Likewise, if knowledge is impossible, inquiry is no virtue and its protection has no point.

That liberty is a means to inquiry also assumes that inquiry is both a public and a social process. It is a public process in the sense that ideas and arguments can be assessed by known and objective standards. One opinion is not as good as another and there are ways of finding out which are which. If inquiry is not public in this sense, it again has no point and no institutions for its protection are called for. Inquiry is a social activity in the sense that social processes are important to it. Arguments for academic freedom assume that inquiry is served by institution-alizing the processes of criticism and debate. We quite reason-ably refuse to place much confidence in an idea until it has survived and been refined by such institutionalized processes.

There is no doubt an individual side to inquiry. Questions of liberty and inquiry, however, assume that some institutional arrangements facilitate inquiry and others do not. They are sensible questions only to the extent that inquiry is a social process.

Thus, claims about the role of liberty in promoting inquiry assume some basic things about the nature of inquiry and the character of knowledge. They also raise difficult problems, particularly problems concerning legitimate and illegitimate roles for intellectual and political authority. By intellectual authority I mean the authority that stems from intellectual competence, from being in a position to know or judge. By political authority I mean the authority that stems from being the duly constituted representative of some legitimate political process. Congressmen and Members of Parliament are instances of political authorities. Professors, lecturers and teachers are, it is to be hoped, instances of intellectual authority, although when they are employed by governments they are political authorities as well. One should never forget that educational institutions can be arms of the state.

Any reasonable view of free inquiry must give some legitimate role to each form of authority. If we do not attach some authority to intellectual competence we shall not know who is entitled to teach or which of the numerous papers submitted to professional journals should be published. If we err in one direction here, we shall make inquiry captive to an intellectual establishment. If we err in the other, we shall drown it in a cacophony of undifferentiable opinion. Likewise we must attach some weight to political authority. Educational institutions serve a number of public purposes in democratic societies. They are supposed to produce citizens who are politically and economically competent. Democratic societies require a rational and educated citizenry. Universities also produce knowledge, much of which is targeted to various public needs, and they train people to perform various public tasks. It is surely reasonable that the state should be entitled to oversee these tasks. But it is no small task to discover ways to protect the public's interest in education while preserving the intellectual freedom of those who teach and learn in these institutions. Here to err in one direction will make thought captive to economic or political interests. To err in the other, is to fail to protect the society's legitimate interests in education.

These questions are among the most difficult and most important in the philosophy of education. We have just emerged from a period when there was much emphasis on the role of freedom in education. We are now reacting to the innovations of that period. I believe much of the failure of freedom-oriented innovations resulted from their inability to solve the problem of finding a role for intellectual competence. I have been told of one case where a teacher, inspired by the need of students for freedom and the undesirability of teachers imposing their views on children, took a vote on the location of Rome. The class democratically located it in France. A view that treats standards of rationality and intellectual competence as obstacles to the student's freedom to learn will fail to educate every bit as much as a view that imposes some orthodoxy.

We are also living in a period in which the desire to make education 'accountable' is leading to increased efforts by governments and administrators to discover effective ways to manage education. While we are making education accountable, we need to be careful that we do not make it accountable in a way that inhibits the capacity of individuals to hold views contrary to what is currently seen as in the public interest. Here is a nest of difficult problems. Historically, the demand for academic freedom has been expressed as forbidding attaching penalties to the expression of unpopular opinion. Currently, however, this is not the most troublesome of the ways in which freedom of expression is likely to be restricted. Let us imagine, for example, a case where the authorities who are responsible for training teachers decide on some major 'reform' in the process. What is apt to happen to those involved in teacher training who object to the reform? It is unlikely that they will be fired or directly repressed. They may even achieve some success in expressing their views in professional journals. It is also the case that they will begin to have a smaller role in teacher preparation, and as a consequence, they will have less access to the rewards and privileges that flow to those who succeed in serving identified needs. And it is likely that agreement with the operational view of teacher training will become a criterion of hiring. Those who dissent will, thus, not be replaced. If the 'reform' endures, the particular species of dissenter will become extinct in the university community.

It seems then that there are other ways of imposing an orthodoxy short of direct attacks on dissenters. The above process surely does reduce the intellectual wares that can be sold in the marketplace of ideas. It is also arguable that this kind of process is necessary and desirable. If administrators have no means whereby they can entice faculty to support new efforts and programmes, how can they be expected to be accountable to the public?

The problems of freedom and authority in education are, thus, numerous and far from solved. Furthermore, we shall do ourselves a disservice if we deal with this problem by means of clichés about freedom and learning. We need instead to take a hard look at both the process of inquiry and its social role. Only then will we be able successfully to ascribe legitimate roles to liberty and authority in education.

Schools and universities are not only educational institutions, they are agents of the state. In most parts of the world schools and universities are financed and operated by some governmental agency. Even when that is not the case schools are heavily regulated by the government. Moreover, in most democratic societies governments do far more than make provisions for an educational system. They also compel their citizens below a certain age to avail themselves of this education. The existence of publicly financed, operated or regulated schools in itself involves significant encroachments on the liberty of citizens. The wealth of citizens is appropriated by the state to pay for schooling, and individuals are compelled to send their children to state-operated or state-regulated schools.

It should be instructive concerning the liberties students should expect in schools to look at some of the arguments for this kind of coercion. If we may assume the rule that individuals should be free to do as they choose unless reasons can be given for limiting this liberty, we may make progress in determining the extent of freedom permissible in education by looking at the areas in which coercion is permissible. Presumably in education, as well as other social institutions, the end of the state's right to coerce is the beginning of the individual's sphere of liberty.

Milton Friedman suggests a framework in which state

involvement in education can be justified:

> . . . governmental intervention into education can be rationalized on two grounds. The first is the existence of substantial 'neighbour-hood effects,' i.e., circumstances under which the action of one individual imposes significant costs on other individuals for which it is not feasible to make him compensate them, or yields significant gains to other individuals for which it is not feasible to make them compensate him – circumstances that make voluntary exchange impossible. The second is the paternalistic concern for children and other irresponsible individuals.[4]

Friedman illustrates the application of this.

> A stable and democratic society is impossible without a minimum degree of literacy and knowledge on the part of most citizens and without widespread acceptance of some common set of values. In consequence, the gain from the education of a child accrues not only to the child or to his parents but also to other members of the society.[5]

This framework for justifying government involvement in education requires a number of comments. Note first that this view is quite similar to the intuitive arguments about liberty with which I began this chapter. It is the fact that if an enterprise has consequences for someone else, consequences that they cannot voluntarily elect to undergo or avoid, that enterprise becomes a matter of public concern, which justifies governmental involvement. Government is thus legitimately involved in education when and to the extent that education produces consequences that are shared in by others in such a way that this sharing cannot be voluntarily elected.

Friedman adds to this criterion for governmental involvement a second, paternalistic concern for children. Here I believe he is mistaken. Competence can reasonably be a condition of liberty. Paternalism is thus a reasonable course of action toward those who are incapable of competent self-governance. But it is one thing to entitle parents to regulate the conduct of their minor children. It is quite another to vest that power in the state. At the very least, Freidman's argument requires another premise.

What is of most interest in Friedman's argument, however, is that it carries the clear implication that government involve-

ment in education should be limited to those cases where there
are clear neighbourhood effects. Government involvement
beyond this point can be regarded as an unjustified intrusion on
the individual's right to exercise choice in education and thus as
a violation of personal liberty.

US federal courts appear to have adopted a view quite similar
to this in deciding cases concerning the limits that can be placed
on the right of governments to compel students to attend school.
In one notable case, *Yoder v Wisconsin*, the US Supreme Court
set out to determine whether the State of Wisconsin could
enforce its compulsory education laws against its Amish
minority, whose religious commitment to a simple agricultural
life seemed to preclude formal education after the age of 12.
Here the Court reasoned that the Amish's right to the free
exercise of their religious convictions was a basic liberty that
could be overruled only by some compelling state interest. They
thus set out to determine what the public interest in education
was, ultimately deciding that it resided in the political and
economic competence of its citizens. These interests they
subsumed under the broader label, citizenship. The Court then
reasoned that the state's interest in producing competent
citizens would be sufficient to overrule the Amish's religious
liberty, were the two in fact to be found to conflict. But they also
found that the Amish seem to succeed admirably in making
good citizens of their children without the aid of formal
schooling. The Court thus enjoined Wisconsin from enforcing
its compulsory education laws against the Amish.

The legal framework in analysing this case is similar to that of
Friedman in that it is assumed that a government may interfere
with the liberty of its citizens only when there is some significant
public interest at stake. It is the neighbourhood effects of
schooling that are seen as the basis of a government's right to
compel attendance.

What is most important to notice about these arguments is
that little depends on the fact that the institution to which they
are applied is a school, that the public interests at stake are
educational interests, or that the liberties at stake are connected
to some educational objective. The conceptual framework
applied to schools here could be used to analyse any social
institution. In effect, the framework requires that the liberties of

the citizens of a state be balanced against the general public welfare. Nothing about this view requires the particular liberties involved to have any connection with educational goals. They may, as do freedom of speech or inquiry. But other liberties, such as freedom of religion, freedom from unreasonable search and seizure, or the right to privacy, will also be analysed in this framework. The connection of these rights to any educational goals is not apparent.

It follows that people may have rights and liberties in educational institutions to which the fact that the institution is an educational one is quite accidental. Thus, if we are to have a reasonable view of liberty to apply to educational institutions, we shall have to look further than to the connection of liberty with learning or inquiry. We shall also have to look at the broader framework of arguments about freedom that apply to social institutions generally. Moreover, we may need to ask whether there are any points at which the general framework of rights and liberties a society applies to its institutions can conflict with the educational goals of schools. *Yoder v Wisconsin* is a case in point. Part of Wisconsin's defence of its right to enforce its compulsory education laws against the Amish was that the education it sought to provide Amish children would substantially enhance the freedom of these children to make reasoned choices concerning their future. Failure to provide such an education commits these children to their parents' way of life by default. Surely providing children with the intellectual competence to make reasoned choices is a worthy educational objective – one that, in this case, is foreclosed by the protections afforded to the Amish's religious liberty. Here we have a sharp conflict between important educational and non-educational values, each of which can be defended in the name of liberty. In such conflicts, much will depend on how we see education fitting in to a broader range of social rights and obligations.

If we are going to resolve such issues, we shall have to have a general view of how rights are to be justified. When we have conflicts between various kinds of rights, how do we choose? What is our final court of appeal? To address this question, I want to sketch here two general philosophical positions that can be used to argue rights of a variety of sorts.

Let us call the first point of view *consequentialism*. Consequentialism holds that rights are justified in terms of their consequences. Its opposite, non-consequentialism, holds that rights are justified in ways other than in terms of their consequences. A consequentialist view, therefore, will proceed by identifying a good or class of goods that a society should attempt to pursue. The rights that that society extends to individuals will be defended by showing that such rights tend to maximize the particular class of goods at issue.

Consider, for example, one consequentialist line of argument for free speech and free inquiry. The dominant consequentialist view is usually referred to as utilitarianism. It maintains that just institutions are those that promote the greatest happiness for the greatest number. Rights and liberties thus need to be defended in terms of the capacity to promote the general happiness of society. Free speech might be held to do this in a number of ways. Perhaps being allowed to say whatever pops into one's head itself makes people happy. Perhaps free and open discussion promotes a higher level of competence in decision making, or perhaps free inquiry promotes a higher quality of research, which in turn contributes to the betterment of all our lives. These are paradigm cases of consequentialist arguments.

To illustrate a non-consequentialist argument I shall sketch a position that I shall argue in detail in chapter 6. The argument concerns student rights. Why should a school be obligated to extend the right of free speech to a student who may be presumed to be ignorant and incapable of contributing anything of intellectual value to the discussion of whatever happens to be at issue? Here consequentialist arguments are likely to be at their weakest. If we must justify student rights by showing that student contributions are important to the advancement of knowledge, we may fail, especially if we are talking about younger students. But something else may be involved. I shall argue that extending the right of free speech to students is a way of showing respect for the students' worth and human dignity. Children may not have a great deal to contribute to scholarship. They are, however, persons and as such are entitled to our respect. This duty of respect is discharged in part by our willingness to listen to their views, regardless of the quality of these views. This is a non-consequentialist argument. It argues for free speech not by showing that it is a means to some end that is contingent on it, but by showing that it is a moral duty in its own right in that it is part of the general duty to show respect for persons.

Consequentialist and non-consequentialist arguments are not, of course, mutually exclusive. I shall hold here that non-consequentialist arguments are fundamental – that rights must ultimately be rooted in what it means to be a person and the duties we owe to persons. It does not follow that social institutions cannot be evaluated in terms of their consequences. That an institution or practice has beneficial consequences surely must count in its favour. But it does mean that the consequences of a practice cannot be the only or sole consideration.

The point of this may be seen by considering the case of punishment. Consequentialist arguments may defend punishment as a way of deterring crime or anti-social behaviour. But such an argument cannot be fundamental for the simple reason that it does not require us to punish the guilty or only the guilty. Punishment of innocent people can be equally deterring if only they are believed to be guilty. This argument suggests that while its deterrent effects may be relevant to the justification of punishment, this cannot be the entire story. There must be some more fundamental reason why it is right to punish the guilty and not the innocent, even if punishing the innocent might have beneficial consequences.

The example also suggests two defects with consequentialist arguments: they can be employed to justify acts that are intuitively abhorrent, and they are entirely future oriented. In the first instance, consequentialist arguments will generally justify exploitation if the benefits to the exploiter exceed the harm to the exploited. Few of us, I suspect, would find slavery to be justified if the benefits to the master exceeded the loss to the slave. Nor would we find teaching methods that involved humiliation and intimidation of students justified if student achievement increased as a consequence. These practices violate our sense of humane treatment of individuals and they do so regardless of whether the benefits exceed the harm.

Consequentialist arguments also discount the past in favour of the future. If we are to judge an action by its consequences, we will look only to the future. The past is dead. In the case of punishment, guilt or innocence become relevant to whom we should punish only if it turns out that punishment is effective only when the guilty but not the innocent are punished. Consequentialist argument thus makes the history of guilt or innocence at best accidentally related to punishment. To hold that guilt is more intimately related to punishment is to believe that the past, as well as the future, has moral relevance. That the past is morally relevant is important to more than just punishment. It is a significant factor, for example, in understanding why we should keep our promises or why rewards should be earned. A view that regards the past as morally irrelevant is an insufficient basis for consideration of rights.

In what follows I shall hold that the arguments that justify academic freedom are consequentialist arguments. The freedoms to inquire, to teach and to learn are justified because they advance knowledge and because knowledge is a means to human well-being. But broader civil liberties, those that transcend the bounds of educational situations and in which all persons share, are justified by the fact that human beings are moral agents responsible for their own lives and deserving of respect.

A cogent view of liberty and learning requires a development and integration of these themes. The place to begin is with the epistemological arguments. How is freedom related to inquiry?

# I

# The Epistemology of Liberty

# Liberty and the Authority of Received Ideas

One of the major thrusts in arguments concerning liberty assumes that the primary goals of liberty are intellectual: liberty is supposed to promote inquiry or learning; its virtue is to promote the pursuit of truth. We need not assume here that this is the sole purpose of liberty. It is not. But clearly it is a major one. Moreover, it is the approach to questions of liberty that seems most apt to illuminate the educational setting. Educational institutions, after all, have learning and inquiry among their basic goals.

This approach to questions of liberty and learning leads to a consideration of epistemology and what I have called the epistemological arguments for liberty. Arguments that hold that liberty is a prerequisite of inquiry must assume a view about what inquiry is like, and arguments that hold that liberty is a prerequisite of learning must make assumptions about learning. What assumptions are required? Are they true?

I shall approach the problem by examining a paradox. First, let us put it abstractly. What attitude shall we have toward the set of concepts, theories, ideas and values that we receive from the past? We may view them as obstacles to creative and intelligent thought. If we are to progress intellectually, must we not regard all received ideas as suspect? If children are to grow into free and creative people, must not adults and teachers see their role as helping students form their own views, and does this not require that we liberate students from the dead hand of the past?

On the other hand, concepts, theories and ideas are not only the objects of thought, they are its instruments. We think with

17

them as well as about them. Does this not suggest that we must attach some authority to them, particularly in an educational context? Perhaps students should be expected to be conversant with received ideas before they are entitled to an independent thought. Stephen Toulmin provides a quotable version of the problem:

> Intellectually, also, man is born with the power of original thought, and everywhere this originality is constrained within a particular conceptual inheritance; yet, on closer inspection, these concepts too turn out to be the necessary instruments of effective thought.[1]

Note that this tension concerning the status of received opinion has numerous expressions in contemporary educational institutions. Universities commonly give eloquent expression to the virtues of free and open inquiry. Moreover, they have constructed institutions intended to promote it. Tenure, for example, is supposed to provide the kind of job security required if professors and lecturers are to be free to advocate new and potentially unpopular ideas.

On the other hand, it cannot be denied that much of what goes on in educational institutions, even among university faculties, gives silent testimony to the authority of received ideas. Tolerance is rarely extended to students whose intellectual novelties involve revisions of physics or who engage in 'creative' arithmetic. Nor do universities hesitate to deny tenure to those whose arguments or viewpoints are regarded as incompetent. No respectable university would have an astrologer in the astronomy department no matter how good an astrologer the person was. When such judgements are made it is usual to distinguish between evaluating the competence of a person's work and disagreeing with the positions taken in that person's work. At the same time, it is frequently difficult to differentiate a person's views and the intellectual competence exhibited in defending them. Certainly people whose articles are rejected by journals or whose contracts are not renewed frequently feel that their work has been rejected because of its departure from orthodoxy, rather than its competence. Nor are such sentiments uncommon among students, on whom the potential threat to grade or career for disagreeing with the teacher is rarely lost.

Educational institutions thus behave in ways designed to

promote free inquiry. They also behave in ways that assume that received ideas have some kind of authority. The legitimacy of much of what we do in contemporary educational institutions depends a great deal on the kind of authority we are willing to ascribe to received ideas.

Perhaps, then, we might begin by looking at the case for the authority of received opinion. The argument I shall make here depends substantially on the following point: *the things that I have been loosely referring to as received ideas or that Toulmin calls a conceptual inheritance are not simply the objects of thought; they are the means or instruments of thought.* If this is the case, then one who understands intellectual liberty in a way that requires the immediate rejection of any received ideas has committed an absurdity. For such a person has proposed to have not an open mind, but an empty one. Such an individual has proposed to engage in thought while rejecting the means of thinking.

We might illustrate the point of this claim by imagining a society that responded to the belief that their tools were not the best imaginable and all might be improved by throwing their tools away, only to discover that they had nothing left with which to make better tools. A society can use some of its tools to make better ones. It cannot dispose of all of its tools at once. Likewise, a society can use some of its received ideas to criticize, investigate and improve others. It cannot doubt everything at once. We must grant received ideas at least some provisional authority.

Giving precise content to these sentiments will require a modest venture into epistemology. I shall proceed here by developing a contrast between what I call traditional empiricism and one set of recent views, which I shall represent by means of the views of Thomas Kuhn. This contrast will help focus the issue of the role of concepts in inquiry and learning and thereby give us an approach to the issue of the authority of concepts. Here I should warn the reader that I shall develop an old and extreme variant of empiricism. The point is to make clear what follows from certain epistemological commitments. There are more adequate versions of empiricism. They have the virtue of being more adequate views of inquiry and the defect of being poor expository devices.

*Traditional empiricism can be expressed as the view that knowledge is obtained by an unbiased systematic examination of experience.* The notion that the examination of nature should be unbiased is often understood as meaning that we should approach the observation of nature without any preconceived ideas of what we shall find. To be a good observer thus means to be an atheoretical observer. That our observation of nature should be systematic expresses the idea that there is something that can be described as *the scientific method.* Empiricist accounts of scientific method differ, but have this in common: the scientific method consists in a set of rules or procedures that enable us to construct warranted generalizations on the basis of systematically collected observations and experiments. Empiricists have usually held that knowledge consists in identifying regularities in experience. Scientific method thus specifies the conditions under which we are entitled to draw general conclusions concerning some regularity in experience from the observation of its instances.

Experience has a special place in the hearts and minds of empiricists. For traditional empiricism it has been important that experience is more than just the evidence for our ideas. It is the source of them. Not only do we check our ideas against experience, we abstract them from experience. Learning or discovery is a matter of *seeing* the general in the particular. Concepts occur as a consequence of experience. They are justified by further experience.

Experience is, thus, the foundation and cornerstone of knowledge. Moreover, empiricists have held, if experience is to play this role in knowing, it must have some special properties. Chief among these is that experience must be certain. Empiricists have wanted to hold that the source of human error resides in drawing incorrect or unwarranted inferences from experience, but not in experience itself. Experience itself is given and immediate. It is what it is regardless of our ideas and interpretations of it. We cannot be mistaken about it. Even the proverbial drunk who sees the pink elephant errs not in the claim that he *sees* a pink elephant, but in the *inference* that a real pink elephant is the cause of his experience. He does *see* a pink elephant. Experience is infallible, judgement is not.

Most of these commitments of traditional empiricism,

particularly the emphasis on theory-neutral observation of experience, are captured in the traditional empiricist motto, 'There is nothing in the mind that was not first in the senses'. This strictly commits empiricists to the view that all knowledge can be constructed by the individual on the basis of accumulated experience without the benefit of prior concepts. The idea that inquiry is atheoretical is not merely something traditional empiricists happened to hold. It is an inference from empiricism's central commitment.

These commitments have some noteworthy implications for the issue of the authority of received opinion and for intellectual liberty generally. Most important, so far as inquiry is concerned, it is hard to see that traditional empiricism assigns any authority to received opinion. Inquiry is supposed to be unbiased, conducted without preconceived ideas. Opinions, received or otherwise, have no role in the process of inquiry. Received opinion is, thus, purely and simply something to be liberated from. It is the source of prejudice and error. For empiricists the fundamental role of intellectual liberty is its capacity to free thought from the weight of tradition and allow inquiry to attend to experience.

There is a second more oblique connection between traditional empiricism and intellectual liberty. *Empiricism tends to undermine the standing of any intellectual elite. It makes knowledge potentially more democratic.* In doing so it suggests that intellectual forums ought to be as open as possible. New ideas, after all, may come from anywhere or anyone. Conversely, any authority wielded by any intellectual elite is illegitimate authority.

There are two reasons why empiricism suggests that inquiry can be a democratic process. First, a social corollary of the claim that received opinion lacks any authority in inquiry is the claim that those who possess received opinion also lack authority in inquiry. The right of anyone to stand in judgement over the ideas of another must be rooted in their possession of some body of knowledge that gives its possessor superior judgement. If there are not such authoritative ideas, neither can there legitimately be authoritative individuals so far as thought is concerned.

The second reason is that empiricism supports the view that human beings are roughly equal in their intellectual capacity.

Because of the strong emphasis on experience in learning, empiricists have been inclined to see differences among individuals as a function of differences in experience. Empiricists are environmentalists.

Empiricism thus weighs strongly against any form of intellectual elitism or authority. No one is in a position to exercise intellectual authority by virtue of either superior knowledge or superior innate ability. Moreover, the basis of inquiry – experience – is available to everyone. The empiricist has little need of experts. Everyone can be his own expert. Empiricism is the stuff of which intellectual democracy and tolerance are made.

Empiricism does, however, generate some difficulties for standard views of intellectual liberty. Most importantly, it makes it difficult to understand the role of criticism and debate in inquiry. Many of those who wish to defend intellectual liberty do so because they believe that criticism is a central component of the pursuit of truth. Criticism is necessary if we are to refine our ideas or see their weaknesses. Intellectual liberty is supposed to protect and promote criticism.

But if criticism is to have a point, we must make some assumptions about what inquiry is like. We must assume at the least that we have something to learn from the ideas and opinions of other people, and that we are liable to mistakes such that the corrective role of other people is important. Traditional empiricism, however, tends to diminish the importance both of what we have to learn from others and of the corrective role of others in inquiry. Empiricism does, of course, suggest that we have something to learn from others. Other people have experiences, and they can report these experiences to us. We can, thus, profit from what others have seen and learned. But this is a minimal view of the role of others in inquiry. The sharing of experience is not criticism. It does not explain the role of counter-argument. Equally important, it does not account for the extent to which we can learn from others, not so much because they have had experiences that differ from ours, but because they are able to see, interpret or judge a common experience differently. To enter into a discussion with another person concerning a common experience hoping to learn thereby assumes that that person possesses a point of view, an idea or some piece of knowledge that we do not possess that can contribute to our understanding or interpretation of experience.

Empiricism will have difficulty making sense of this process. To share points of view, rather than experiences, with others assumes that ideas have a role in inquiry. It assumes we need to interpret our experiences in the light of acquired wisdom, and it assumes that experience is one thing and its coherent interpretation is another. Traditional empiricism, however, denies these claims. Ideas are not resources for understanding new ideas; they are sources of bias and distortion. For empiricists, an open mind is an empty mind. Moreover, correct interpretation of experience is seen by empiricists as largely a matter of attending to experience systematically and carefully. Theory construction is a matter of stating in general form the patterns or regularities seen in experience. It is not a matter of constructing or creating a viewpoint that makes sense of experience. Experience is regarded as wearing its generalities on its sleeves. They are found by careful looking, not created by careful thinking. Given these views it is hard to see that empiricism suggests much of a role for learning from others in inquiry.

The role of criticism is similarly small. Presumably, criticism is directed at mistakes. So we can understand the role of criticism by asking about the kinds of mistakes there are to be made. Empiricism presents a limited class of mistakes. Experience itself is indubitable; it is not the source of errors. Errors arise in interpretation, not perception. For empiricists, interpreting experience is a matter of discovering regularities by following the procedures of the scientific method and avoiding seduction by prior conception. Empiricism thus suggests two sources of error. The first is bias: one can allow prior conceptions to corrupt one's objectivity. The second is methodological sloppiness: one can err by departing from the rules of scientific thought.

Again, we need not dispute the claims that people can be biased and sloppy, but this view of mistakes is narrow and leads to a narrow view of the point of criticism. It ignores the central fact that criticism usually functions as the means whereby current ideas are brought to bear to assess new ones. Criticism does far more than detect bias or methodological sloppiness. It points out that proposed ideas can be inconsistent with something else we know, that they can fail to consider some important and relevant matter, that they can be expressed in better ways, or interpreted in a different light. Such roles for criticism again make assumptions that traditional empiricists deny. They assume that current ideas have a role in inquiry and that interpretation is more than simply reading generalizations off the surface of experience.

A corollary of the restricted roles empiricism assigns to dialogue and criticism is that empiricists are unlikely to appreciate the role of communities of scholars or simply of communities in inquiry. If criticism is highly valued, so must be critics. If it is important that we learn from the ideas of others, there must be others from whose ideas we can learn. If we do not value dialogue or criticism, there is little reason to value the contribution of other people in inquiry. Empiricism is thus predisposed to see inquiry as an individualistic, rather than a collective, enterprise.

Empiricism generates another issue. Empiricists have seen received opinion as the source of bias and error and have sought to liberate inquiry from the tyranny of the past and focus it on experience. In historical terms such a view had a great deal of attractiveness during the period when the natural sciences were emerging, particularly when their emergence was actively resisted by the church and by the civil authorities. When extant received opinions are the results of the speculations of medieval philosophers and theologians and when these opinions are arrayed against the emerging sciences and backed by the sword and the stake, a doctrine that sees received opinion as nothing more than accumulated bias and whose motto is 'Don't think, look!' will have obvious appeal. We must also ask, however, about the stance we should take concerning received opinion when it includes the products of science. Surely empiricists are not going to see the products of the empirical sciences as so many potential sources of bias.

No doubt they will not, but neither should they see them as substantially contributing to further inquiry. Empiricism, rather, seems to suggest that we should view the products of scientific inquiry in the way in which squirrels view acorns. They are things to be stored up one at a time. Storing away one acorn does not have very much to do with finding the next. That the acorn is a good acorn, that it is not rotten or diseased, makes it a good one to find, but does not help in finding the next. Likewise with the products of science. They are products, but not the means, of further inquiry. One simply squirrels them away. Knowledge grows by accumulation, rather like a pile of nuts. If some received opinion is the product of science, that does not give it a more central role in inquiry. Nor does it alter the point of intellectual liberty, except perhaps to lessen the need for it.

We can now summarize the view of intellectual liberty to which traditional empiricism leads. *The central characteristic of empiricism's concept of intellectual liberty is that it is anti-traditional and anti-elitist. It sees inquiry as an individualistic process of learning from experience that needs protection from both received opinion and intellectual elites. At the same time, empiricism tends to divorce intellectual liberty from dialogue and criticism. It lacks a sense of the role of discussion and debate and of intellectual communities in inquiry. These features of empiricism's concept of intellectual liberty have common roots. They stem from empiricism's rejection of a major role for current concepts in inquiry. Received opinion has no authority.*

Empiricism and its view of liberty and intellectual authority has some obvious implications for education and for teaching and learning. It will diminish the emphasis on transmitting received opinion and increase the emphasis on experience. It can easily lead to the rejection of any insistence by educators that students should master some extant viewpoint. It will tend to diminish the teacher's authority insofar as that authority resides in subject matter expertise. Empiricism will also suggest that learning is an individual, rather than a collective, matter. It will emphasize the quality of experience over the quality of human resources available to students. Empiricism will also tend to divorce scientific method from scientific concepts. Insofar as education aims to make students rational, this can be understood as teaching them to follow the steps of a method that is neutral as regards subject matter, a procedure that in principle can be learned without learning the content of any science. Learning any special content will simply be a matter of efficiency. It is easier to learn what is known from someone else than to discover it for oneself. But such content should not be expected to make the student more intellectually capable. Rationality inheres in method, not content.

Empiricism thus has implications for education that parallel those for inquiry. It is anti-traditional and anti-elitist. Stated in an extreme form it can make subject matter and the attempt to transmit it appear illegitimate. It will prefer experience to concepts and will have no role for intellectual authority in learning.

This version of empiricism has been subjected to a sustained and largely successful critique for the better part of this century. This critique, I shall argue, has among its consequences a much enhanced view of the authority of received opinion. This view is of considerable interest for our understanding of intellectual liberty.

The traditional empiricist's view of the role of prior concepts in inquiry has been regarded as suspect for some time. One standard argument holds that traditional empiricism is defective in that it fails to recognize the role of theory in guiding research. If one is going to collect experience, one must at least have some idea of what to look for. Inquiry is not simply a random observation of the world. There is, after all, an almost infinite number of things to be looked at. Research requires a planned and systematic collection of *relevant* data. How shall we know what is relevant without a theory? Biologist Sir Peter Medawar, in arguing this point, provides a unique illustration from the correspondence of Charles Darwin:

> Almost thirty years ago there was much talk that geologists ought only to observe and not theorize; and I well remember someone saying that at this rate a man might as well go into a gravel pit and count the pebbles and describe the colours. How odd it is that anyone should not see that all observation must be for or against some view if it's to be of any service.[2]

Darwin here suggests that the *role of theory in inquiry is to guide observation, while the role of observation is to test theory*. In more recent philosophy of science, this idea has been expressed as the claim that science proceeds by what Karl Popper calls a process of conjecture and refutation. The scientist begins an investigation with a conjecture – a theoretical guess designed to account for some phenomenon. The next step is to develop the empirical consequences of this conjecture. The scientist reasons, 'If my guess is correct then experience ought to be a certain way and not another.' Then, having deduced what experience should be like if the theory is correct, the scientist will go and make the required observations. If the empirical predictions derived from the theory are confirmed by experience, then the scientist may provisionally continue to subscribe to the theory and to use it as a tool of further inquiry. If the predictions are not confirmed by experience, the theory is refuted and the objective scientist will abandon it and try another. This view of science is commonly called the hypothetico-deductive method.

Consider a simple example. My African violet is dying. A plant pathologist friend, after inspecting the plant (and knowing its owner), has offered the conjecture that the plant is suffering from lack of water. Certain predictions follow, among which are that if I begin to water the plant regularly, it will revive. If I begin to water my plant and it revives, that is evidence that my friend's conjecture was correct. (It is not decisive evidence: perhaps my watering drowned the insects that were eating the roots of my plant.) If the plant continues its downward spiral my friend's hypothesis will be refuted.

This view rejects traditional empiricism at several notable points. Initially, it denies that concepts or theories emerge from observation in the simple way suggested by empiricism. Theories or hypotheses are normally guesses we bring to experience. They are not somehow read off the surface of the phenomena being investigated. The central role of experience in inquiry is to confirm or reject theories.

These modifications of empiricism also alter the concept of bias and enhance the authority of received ideas. On this view of inquiry, bias is not understood as approaching experience with something in mind. Rather, it is a matter of refusing to accept the verdict of experience on the theories we bring to it. It is the researcher who refuses to abandon a pet theory once it has been refuted who lacks objectivity. It is not how we approach experience, but how we leave it, that is decisive for objectivity.

This view enhances the authority of received opinion in the sense that it suggests that at any given time there will be a theory or set of theories that are the current objects of investigation. These theories will substantially determine, at least for academic inquiry, what is the relevant direction of inquiry. To that extent theories can also define who is engaged in relevant inquiry. Knowledge of current theory is thus a prerequisite for participation in the intellectual life of any community of scholars.

It is important to note, however, that this view indicates that current theory can determine the relevance, but not the competence, of any inquiry. Presumably, most extant theories are extant because they will have survived their initial tests. A surviving theory of any scope will generate a large class of empirical predictions. As these predictions are confirmed they will lend credence to the theory and increase the incentive to test its remaining predictions. On hypothetico-deductive views this is presumably how theories gain some authority over the direction of inquiry. But such theories do not define intellectual competence. Hypothetico-deductive views still assume there is something called 'the scientific method', which consists of the abilities to generate hypotheses, deduce their empirical consequences and test them. These processes are understood in such a way that the required capacities are largely mathematical or logical. The theories themselves play no role in defining such abilities. What one needs to know to think scientifically is still logically independent of what is being thought about.

It is also the case that hypothetico-deductive views regard experience as certain. It is given, immediate, and is what it is independent of the theories or interpretations we bring to it. Indeed, it is the incorrigible objectivity of experience that permits it to be the final court of appeal for our theories. Our theories may tell us where to look and what to look for, but they do not otherwise determine what we see. Ideas are, thus, not authoritative for having experience.

The upshot of these considerations is that *hypothetico-deductive views do enhance the authority of received opinion. Extant theories are authoritative in determining the relevant direction of inquiry and observation. They are not, however, authoritative in the far more fundamental sense of significantly infecting the sense of method. The processes of deducing the consequences of a theory and testing them are conceived independently of extant theory. Indeed, objectivity is seen as requiring this sort of independence of method and content. Received opinion is not yet very authoritative for thought.*

More recent views change this situation considerably. Here my vehicle will be the views of Thomas Kuhn as expressed largely in *The Structure of Scientific Revolutions*.[3] It should be noted at the outset, however, that my purpose here is not Kuhn exegesis. The view of Kuhn I shall generate is formulated for expository purposes. Perhaps it should be regarded as a Kuhnian view, rather than as Kuhn's view. As to its implications for educational authority, what I shall say is what I believe follows from this Kuhnian view, which is not always what Kuhn has said.

Kuhn regards mature sciences as dominated by some intellectual achievement, some set of concepts, which he terms a paradigm. A paradigm serves a far broader role in Kuhn's views than theories in hypothetico-deductive views. A paradigm serves to set the problems that a science must solve, it suggests the directions to be pursued in approaching these problems, and it indicates what counts as a solution to them. Indeed, Kuhn in a very literal way seems to regard a paradigm as the means whereby scientists *see* the piece of the world with which they deal. A paradigm for Kuhn is thus intimately involved in every phase of inquiry.

The role of paradigms in inquiry can be made clearer by means of an example. Let us assume that the theory of evolution functions as a paradigm for many areas of inquiry in biology.

The first point to make is that paradigms generate problems to be solved, rather than simply generating empirical predictions. This is particularly true of evolution. Evolution, for example, requires that species have developmental histories. It does not inform us what these histories are. That is something that must be constructed. The tools of reconstruction can vary from palaeontology to organic chemistry. Evolution does not demand that any species has any particular history. It does, however, place constraints on the kinds of development a species can undergo. It requires, for example, that change be gradual and adaptive. All large-scale changes must be the result of a series of smaller changes, each of which is adaptive of itself. Such requirements function both as criteria for the kinds of species-histories that will be acceptable – histories that involve the instantaneous emergence of entire new organs will be ruled out – and to generate additional problems. Cases where some organ or capacity would be dysfunctional until it was fully matured become challenges. Half a wing seems worse than none. How could birds gradually evolve then? Human language or thought seems a fully developed species capacity that is not approximated in animals. What kind of gradual development might such structures or capacities have had? Paradigms thus generate problems to be solved and suggest the criteria for their solution.

The claim that paradigms are ways of seeing the world is particularly important. Kuhn holds that people with different paradigms do more than interpret the world differently. What people see in the world depends not just on what is there to be seen, but on the concepts people see with. Two people looking in the same place but with different concepts can see different things. The standard illustration of this point is a gestalt figure.

Here what one sees – a duck or a rabbit – depends on the concept one brings to the experience. *Perception is concept-embedded*!

Consider another biological example. There is a famous case where the percentage of dark and light members of a certain species of moth changed as the amount of soot put out by local industry changed. During the period when soot increased or was high the percentage of dark moths in the population was high. When the local industry cleaned up its production process, the percentage of light coloured moths increased. Someone who approaches this phenomenon with the theory of natural selection can *see* these changes as instances of adaptation. Presumably, the colouration of the moths serves to make them more or less visible to predators. As soot darkened the background in the environment that proved to the advantage of the dark moths, which increased in number in comparison with the more visible and more vulnerable light moths. When this situation was reversed, the light part of the population increased. A person with the proper theory can see these facts as adaptation. A person without the proper theory cannot.

This, I believe, is a most profound point. *Not only does it seem that people with different concepts see different things, but it also seems that concepts are a precondition of having some experiences.* Kuhn thus seems to reverse the relations between concepts and theory as they are understood by traditional empiricism. Empiricism assumes that concepts are somehow abstracted from or constructed out of experience. Kuhn, however, argues that concepts are sometimes prerequisite to seeing. One must learn to see.

Scientific inquiry for Kuhn has two quite distinct phases. The most common phase, which Kuhn refers to as normal science, is the process of working on the problems generated by a paradigm (Kuhn describes normal science as puzzle-solving). A second phase, however, occurs when the paradigm itself is in doubt. Paradigms are not directly refuted by experience. They generate puzzles and problems, not predictions. There are no firm empirical consequences of a paradigm that can be at odds with actual observations. Paradigms do, however, generate approaches to problems. These approaches can be more or less successful in leading to solutions. The inability of a paradigm to lead to solutions for the problems it generates can ultimately lead to the rejection of a paradigm. If a paradigm generates such a set of what Kuhn calls anomalies and if it has a competitor, scientists may come to regard its competitor as offering more fruitful approaches to research and shift their allegiance to the new paradigm. Kuhn refers to this process as revolutionary science.

It is worth noting here that while Kuhn sometimes sounds as though a paradigm shift is virtually an act of faith akin to a religious conversion, in fact the selection of a new paradigm is not an arbitrary matter. Most significantly, a new paradigm should meet the basic test of appearing to solve (or eliminate) the problems generated by its predecessor. Thus, even the selection of a new paradigm is a process regulated by some extant set of concepts and problems. Paradigms are not chosen in an intellectual vacuum.

What view of intellectual authority does Kuhn's view lead to? Here we need not adopt all of the features of Kuhn's view of inquiry. I do, however, want to accept as given (for purposes of the current argument) several features of Kuhn's viewpoint. Having put these in less Kuhnian terms, we can then look at the view of intellectual authority they require. I want, then, to accept the following epistemological claims:

(1) *Problems are generated by current concepts.* Intellectual problems do not simply emerge from experience. They are, rather, more likely to be the product of a discrepancy between the intellectual expectations generated by our current concepts and our actual current capacity to explain experience in terms of these concepts.

(2) *Solutions to problems are judged by means of current concepts.* Proposed solutions to problems need to do more than simply explain or predict the phenomena. They need to do so in ways that current concepts regard as a successful form of explanation and in ways that are consistent with other knowledge.

(3) *Concepts are a precondition of experience.* Seeing is something we do with ideas as well as senses. We cannot see what we cannot conceive. Moreover, people who approach the world with different concepts will see it differently.

We need one additional idea that has not yet been explicitly mentioned, but that is implicit in what has been said.

(4) *Current concepts are a product of a history of conceptual development.* Current concepts are a product of a history of attempts to understand the world and the modification of concepts in the light of their inadequacies. Current concepts may not be perfect, but they are rarely arbitrary or altogether unreasonable. There is a reasonable presumption concerning received views that they are received because they have had some success in accounting for some range of experience, they have survived over their competition and they are products of some degree of testing and refinement. This does not guarantee their truth or their current or continued adequacy. It does make them objects of respect, not to be lightly dismissed.

*These points are effectively summarized in the claim that concepts are not merely the objects or results of thought, but the instruments of thought. How well we can think thus depends not just on how smart we are or on our mastery of something called the scientific method, but on the mastery of the substantive concepts employed in an area of thought and on the quality of these conceptual resources.*

These epistemological views have a number of implications for the authority of received opinions and for educational authority. We can state the basic implications generally in two assertions.

(1) *No idea is beyond challenge.* These epistemological views do not assign final authority to any idea. There is no concept that is so central to our thinking that it is impossible to challenge that idea or to imagine its rejection. In this sense whatever authority ideas have, no idea has any ultimate intellectual authority. There is no single concept without which thought is impossible and no idea that is so certain that its denial must be irrational.

(2) *Some ideas are central to our capacity to think about certain things at certain times.* These ideas, as a consequence, have provisional intellectual and educational authority. No idea is certain. Neither can we challenge or doubt every idea simultaneously. Some ideas in a given discipline at a given time will function as basic tools of thought on that discipline. They will thus have a kind of provisional authority over the intellectual activities of that discipline. They will function as the standards to be employed in judging intellectual work in a discipline and will be authoritative for the education of new practitioners in the discipline.

It is, of course, the second claim that will raise hackles. It has become heretical in modern culture to assign any kind of authority to any idea whatsoever. The view I have suggested will appear undemocratic, elitist and authoritarian – descriptive terms that are hardly among the honorific vocabulary of our age. We are rather inclined instead to take the imagery of the marketplace of ideas as a serious metaphor for our educational institutions. We thus envisage them as smorgasbords or flea markets of intellectual wares among which free rational agents pick and choose as they see fit and where anyone with a novel thought is at liberty to try it out and see if it sells.

But the 'flea market' rendering of the marketplace of ideas is absurd, because ideas are not only the objects of thought, they are the means. If this is true, then intellectual shoppers in such a cognitive flea market face a dilemma. If our shoppers approach an intellectual choice with completely open minds, they cannot make rational choices, for they will lack the means. Ideas are the means of rational choice. On the other hand, if our shoppers come to our cognitive sale with ideas in mind or if our sale has already excluded merchandise regarded as inferior, then they will not be totally free in their choices. The moral of this little metaphor is, I hope, clear: the intellectually uninitiated are in no position to make rational choices; when they are in such a position, some choices – the most important – will already have been made. This dilemma follows quite directly from the view that ideas are tools of thought.

The set of epistemological commitments sketched is, thus, guilty of the charge of intellectual elitism so far as education is concerned. Even if (especially if!) education is viewed as fundamentally concerned with the liberation of the student's mind, it will focus on initiating the student into a set of concepts and ideas that have been found to be effective intellectual tools. The decision as to what these concepts will be is presumably to be made by those who are in a position to identify the best intellectual tools – experts.

These epistemological commitments are also elitist in that they provide some justification for the role that referees play in many forms of intellectual life. A referee is someone who exercises authority over an intellectual product in which authority is rooted in intellectual competence. Journal editors are perhaps a paradigm case. Their role is to judge the merit of scholarly articles. Their authority resides in their ability to allow some work to see the light of day while excluding other work. In making such decisions referees will exert considerable influence over both the direction of intellectual endeavours and over the careers of members of intellectual professions. Indeed, making decisions that affect people's careers is a major part of the role of a referee. The kinds of judgements of intellectual competence that determine who gets published, who gets promoted, who gets a degree, or even who gets what grade, are the major forms of institutional decisions determining intellectual directions and currents.

Indeed, the epistemological views sketched indicate that both inquiry and learning will be rather undemocratic processes. That received ideas have the sort of authority I have ascribed to them indicates that there will be vast differences between the novice and the expert, both in terms of their relative ability to participate competently in an inquiry and in terms of their ability to make rational educational choices. These differences directly result from the fact that the expert has mastered the concepts and principles that govern the process of inquiry and learning, whereas the novice has not. There is, thus, a significant inequality between the expert and the novice. Moreover, this inequality is relevant to the capacity of the respective individuals to make competent judgements about inquiry and learning. Again, this point follows directly from the fact that concepts are the tools of inquiry, not just the objects of inquiry.

To summarize: *the epistemological commitments I have sketched have elitist and undemocratic implications for the conduct of inquiry and of education because they suggest that those who have mastered the concepts of a discipline are uniquely qualified to render competent judgements about inquiry and learning. The authority of ideas leads to the authority of those who possess them over the institution that deals with ideas.*

These epistemological views enable us to make sense of both the process of criticism and debate and the role of intellectual communities. They suggest that criticism and debate are a fundamental part of inquiry and are crucial to the growth of knowledge. They have this consequence largely because they indicate that the interpretation of experience is by no means an easy matter or one that can be clearly settled by additional experience or experimentation. Rather, they suggest that any proposed conceptual innovation must be judged against a whole set of intellectual standards and criteria that are embedded in the current state of a discipline. Such an assessment calls for subtle, complex and frequently difficult judgements. Thus it is crucial that new ideas be subjected to searching criticism. It is only by such a process that the diversity of considerations that can be relevant to judging new ideas is likely actually to be brought to bear on them.

These considerations also indicate the impact of intellectual communities. Intellectual communities tend to be defined by a shared commitment to a view of the world and a set of intellectual standards. Scholars in a field will not agree on everything, but they will to a large extent share a common paradigm. They will be members of an intellectual tradition who at a given moment will have some shared understanding about what the field's outstanding problems are, about how they should be approached, and about what will count as a solution. The fact that many intellectual communities transcend national and cultural differences is testimony to the extent to which they share such a body of assumptions. It is to members of such communities – people who have been initiated into and have mastered the communities' standards – that new ideas are presented for criticism, modification and, ultimately, acceptance or rejection. These institutions provide the forum in which the process of criticism and debate takes place.

Since it is commonly held that a major purpose of liberty is the protection of the process of criticism and debate, these Kuhnian epistemological assumptions generate a demand for intellectual liberty. It is a fundamental feature of institutions that conduct inquiry that they allow scholars to voice their opinions and criticisms freely without fear of suffering for the expression of an unpopular idea. What needs to be noted, however, is the extent to which Kuhnian assumptions generate an elitist version of intellectual liberty; for they easily lead to the view that criticism and debate are activities that have a point only when confined to members of intellectual communities. It is, after all, the members of a given intellectual community who possess a reasonable grasp of the ideas and principles that govern inquiry in their area. They are therefore the individuals who are in a position to contribute to a meaningful debate on an idea and to render judgement on its worth. Kuhn's views thus suggest little reason why the various intellectual liberties should be extended beyond the boundaries of intellectual professions. Freedom seems to be for the competent.

Moreover, as we have already noted, even within intellectual professions Kuhnian views lead to non-democratic views of governance. Power to decide whose opinions are aired or who is to be promoted resides in a professional elite – senior persons whose authority has presumably been earned by a demonstration of superior mastery of and achievement within their field. Kuhnian views tend to justify this sort of elitism in that they suggest that competence to recognize quality work will vary according to attainment.

Kuhnian views also have a distinctive view of the nature of objectivity and bias. Most importantly, objectivity will not be understood as approaching an issue without prior conceptions. Rather, the inquirer will be expected to approach any issue with some substantive views concerning the nature of the question, proper procedures for investigating it, and what is to count as an acceptable conclusion. These assumptions will be rooted in the fundamental theories and concepts of a field. They are not merely subject matter neutral logical rules. Employing such assumptions cannot be a lapse of objectivity, for they define objectivity. The failure to be objective is a failure to view a question as the extant concepts of the field indicate. It is to be motivated by considerations other than those that are part of the field's paradigm. An open mind is not an empty mind. It is one that is governed by the standards of a field.

This does not, of course, mean that the standards of a field cannot change. It does mean, however, that the extent to which a concept has come to be seen as authoritative in a field will be the extent to which it is held immune from criticism. Moreover, the degree to which such authoritative concepts are under criticism is the degree to which it will be unclear exactly what is to count as objectivity in a field. I do not believe that concepts ever should be altogether immune from criticism or that any given concept is ever so central to a field's standards that it cannot be cogently doubted. These nods in the direction of fallibilism should not, however, mislead us about the extent to which the notion of objectivity is substantially defined at any given moment by the concepts that have become authoritative in a field.

We are now in a position where we can summarize the contrasting views on intellectual liberty and authority that result from Kuhnian and from classical empiricist assumptions. Classical empiricism tends to see intellectual liberty as liberty from any intellectual tradition or received opinion. An unbiased inquirer is one who approaches phenomena with no prior conceptions. Moreover, since the competencies required for inquiry are readily available to everyone, empiricists tend to see inquiry in democratic and egalitarian terms. Everyone can be his own scientist. On the other hand, the view of inquiry held by empiricists attaches little importance to the process of criticism and debate or to the role of intellectual communities in the process of inquiry. Inquiry is an individualistic enterprise.

Kuhnian views, on the other hand, emphasize the extent to which inquiry occurs within an intellectual tradition and is guided by certain central concepts. Since mastery of these concepts is seen as essential for engaging in or judging research, Kuhnian views tend to see inquiry as occurring within intellectual communities. Kuhnian views thus tend toward an elitist conception of the governance of inquiry. On the other hand, Kuhnian views have a strong sense of the impact of criticism and debate in inquiry. Intellectual liberty is intended to protect this process.

So far as intellectual liberty is concerned, the crux of the difference is that empiricists will see liberty as liberation from the intellectual past, while Kuhnian views will focus on the process of criticism and debate. These are, of course, different emphases. They are not mutually exclusive. Both views recognize that all ideas are fallible and may need to be revised or changed. Consequently, both views will resist the enforcement of ideas by any means beyond the power of reason, experience and persuasion. Nevertheless, Kuhnian views grant some provisional authority to some current concepts and as a consequence will assign them a central place in inquiry and learning. Again, the crucial fact here is the recognition that current concepts are the tools as well as the products of inquiry.

Thus far, I have defended a Kuhnian point of view. This means that, at the very least, I shall take the authority of some concepts over the processes of inquiry and learning seriously. It also means that my views on these matters may exhibit some elitist tendencies. I have, however, sketched in only the most intuitive fashion what the educational implications of these ideas are. That is, of course, what one might expect. I see these epistemological assumptions as a kind of paradigm themselves. Some of the puzzles to be solved within the confines of these assumptions are those of liberty and learning. Perhaps, then, it would be an opportune time to list some of the questions that a Kuhnian perspective generates.

I shall proceed here by suggesting an initial view concerning educational liberty that might at first seem to follow from a Kuhnian view. Let me suggest two possible implications:

(1) *Intellectual liberty is for the initiated.* The process of criticism and debate has a point only when engaged in by those who have sufficiently internalized the paradigm so as to be able to participate competently in a debate governed by it.

(2) *The governance of inquiry and education should reside largely with an elite who have demonstrated their mastery over the current paradigms.*

In considering the agenda of issues generated by the Kuhnian viewpoint we need to consider more than simply how it is to be implemented. More important is how it is to be qualified. Human affairs differ from questions in the natural sciences in that looking at them from the perspective of a single paradigm is often overly narrow and misleading. Man is not simply economic man, biological man, or psychological man. Certainly he is not merely epistemological man. We must, therefore, be sensitive to the limits of the application of our Kuhnian paradigm and ask about the other perspectives to which it must be accommodated. Consider, then, some questions and issues.

First, what kinds of specific institutions are required to exemplify these abstract views of educational authority and liberty? Particularly, what sorts of authority and what kinds of rights or liberties shall we attach to various members of educational communities?

Secondly, how generalizable are the kinds of epistemological assumptions that have been sketched to the range of intellectual enterprises? Kuhn's views were developed for the natural sciences and rely most heavily on physics. The natural sciences, however, differ from other disciplines in that they have achieved a higher degree of agreement concerning fundamental assumptions. Other disciplines are characterized by sub-communities defined by sharp disagreements concerning the fundamental assumptions under which research is done. In psychology, for example, behaviourists, cognitive psychologists and humanistic psychologists have different views about what psychology is, what its problems are, and how they are to be addressed. Indeed, most of the behavioural and social sciences and the humanities are characterized by multiple 'paradigms' and multiple sub-communities defined by their allegiance to these paradigms. In what sense can a paradigm be said to have any authority under such conditions and what is the consequence of such intellectual confusion for the authority of those institutions whose authority is seen as rooted in the authority of ideas?

Thirdly, to what extent are there legitimate educational goals that go beyond disciplinary goals and to what extent must we accommodate views of educational authority to principles other than those derived from an analysis of the requirements of intellectual enterprises? Schools are frequently asked to promote a host of objectives that go beyond the development and transmission of ideas. They are supposed to promote citizenship, economic development, equality and vocational competence. Such objectives are political objectives, not intellectual ones. It seems reasonable that pursuing them should make schools responsible to the authority of the state as well as to the authority of the intellectually competent. Thus, we must ask about the kinds of rights and duties that can be applied to educational institutions but that do not flow from the epistemological considerations with which we have thus far dealt.

Finally, we must ask more directly about the rights and liberties of the learner. The learner is not simply an aspirant member of an intellectual community. Learners are persons and citizens who may have rights and liberties enforceable within educational institutions quite independently of their role of learner. Moreover, we must also look at the extent to which the learner can be regarded as an inquirer. The arguments I have given to this point may suggest that the role of learner is one of passively acquiring the received wisdom of a field until such time as one has learned enough to have an intelligent opinion. I think, however, that that is far from the case. There are important epistemological considerations that indicate that the role of learner cannot be conceived in such a passive fashion. Indeed, it needs to be recalled that we began the discussion of the authority of ideas with a paradox, one part of which focused on the constraints intellectual traditions place on thought, but the other part of which emphasized the freedom of the learner. We need now to take up the other side of our paradox.

# CHAPTER 3

# The Authority of Ideas and the Students' Right to Autonomy

The ignorance of the person just beginning the study of a subject has a special character. It is not just that the novice is ignorant of the facts and theories of the subject matter; the student is also ignorant of the principles that govern thought about the subject matter. He does not know what the problems of the field are, he does not know what approaches to take to solve a field's problems, and he does not know how to identify a reasonable solution to the problem.

Consider an example. It has been common to introduce the oxidation theory of combustion by means of an experiment in which students are asked to thrust the smouldering end of a stick of wood into an inverted test tube of oxygen. The stick will normally burst into flames. It is then explained that this is because the test tube contains a higher concentration of oxygen than does the air in the classroom and that this oxygen combines with the material in the wood, yielding carbon dioxide and water plus a residue of ash.

What issue is being addressed by this experiment? Note that the explanation is not focused on burning. No account is given of the flame or the heat. My ten-year-old car, like the stick of wood, has undergone considerable oxidation, producing a noticeable residue of iron oxide. It has not, so far as I have been able to see, burst into flame during the process. Why does the oxidation of the wood produce heat and light in large amounts? This is not explained. The reader might ponder the question of what exactly the explanation explains and how the experiment supports the explanation. One should come to the conclusion that the answer

41

is not very obvious. Moreover, with perseverance it may also be observed that a grasp of the issues presupposes a knowledge of such fundamental ideas as the atomic theory of matter and the conservation of matter.

It might also be profitable to ask whether other accounts of the phenomena might be constructed. During the nineteenth century it was widely believed among chemists that heat was a substance that flowed from one place to another. Most phenomena concerned with combustion were explained in terms of the behaviour of this substance, called phlogiston. Could the experiment described above be explained in such terms? Phlogiston theorists were ingenious in explaining apparently difficult phenomena via the theory. Air was necessary for combustion because it was needed to absorb the phlogiston given off. Air in which combustion occurred rapidly (as in our experiment) was dephlogistated air, thus having a great capacity for absorbing phlogiston. Combustion ceased when the air had absorbed its capacity of phlogiston. The real ingenuity of the phlogiston theorists was demonstrated when they were acquainted with the fact that some substances gained in weight when heated. This problem was solved by assigning to phlogiston the property of negative weight. Thus, when the phlogiston was driven out, the object that lost its phlogiston gained weight. The theory has an odd ring to modern ears. But what is wrong with it? Does the combustion experiment described refute it?

I hope that these questions about such a commonplace experiment will be puzzling to the reader. They are meant to suggest how deeply our beliefs about oxygen and combustion are embedded in a complex set of beliefs about physical phenomena, how complex the reasoning is that supports the oxygen theory of combustion, and how unfamiliar most of us are with the principles of reasoning that function in the arguments. Those of us who have been blessed with only an introductory course in chemistry are a long way from being able to reason like a chemist. The novice and the expert differ not just in their knowledge of the facts of chemistry. They differ in their capacity for chemical reasoning. The novice is not in a position to have much of an understanding of even the most simple chemical experiment.

With this as background I want to argue two claims that I believe are central in understanding the students' rights and interests in the pedagogical relationships.

(1)   Students as persons have a right to autonomy. This requires teachers both to give students reasons for what they are asked to believe, within the students' capacity to grasp them, and to teach so as to expand the students' capacity to comprehend and assess reasons.

(2)   A variety of processes, which I shall collectively refer to as reason-giving, is essential to the development of the students' capacity to comprehend and assess the claims of any subject matter.

Persons have the right to autonomy. What does this mean? Fundamentally, it means that people have a *prima facie* right to be self-governing. Autonomy is complex; it contains at least three components. The first is psychological freedom: this is the capacity for independent choice, and it requires the capacity for rational judgement and for self-control. The second component is the right of self-determination in those areas of life that are properly left to the individual's discretion: individuals should have the right to choose their own beliefs and their own lifestyle, and they have a number of other rights that limit a government's or a society's authority over them. Finally, individuals have the right to participate in collective choices.

There is a great deal that might be said about the meaning and justification of these rights that cannot be said here. The following point is crucial. These rights are rooted in the value of moral agency. *Human beings are ends in themselves and are moral agents who are responsible to choose wisely on their own behalf and act justly with respect to others. They are morally responsible for what they choose and what they do.*

A moral agent who is responsible for his choices must demand both the opportunity and the resources to choose wisely. The opportunity for such choices is autonomy. Autonomy in its several forms specifies both the psychological and political preconditions of responsible choice. A person who is not free in these ways cannot freely choose and act.

The resources to choose responsibly are of essentially two sorts. First, responsible choice depends on information and evidence. One cannot consistently demand that a person make a responsible choice and at the same time withhold information relevant to that choice. Here, indeed, is another kind of argument for rights such as free speech or free press, which serve the function of making information freely available for moral agents who require it to decide responsibly. A society that restricts the free flow of information denies to its citizens one of the conditions of responsible choice. In doing so, it in effect expresses a decision to refuse to regard its citizens as responsible moral agents.

Information is not, however, sufficient to allow people to make responsible choices. They must also have the will and ability to do so. Concerning the will to choose responsibly, I shall note only that it seems to me to require such virtues as a regard for and commitment to truth, honesty and fairness. There is, no doubt, much more to say, but I mention these ideals because they are intellectual virtues in the sense that they are pre-supposed by the commitment to have one's choices and actions warranted by available evidence. The central point about the ability to choose responsibly is that having information that provides a satisfactory base for a decision is not the same thing as being able to interpret or judge that information in a reasonable way. This is, of course, the point I have argued at length: concepts are tools. Two people with the same piece of information can differ vastly in terms of their capacity to draw reasonable conclusions from it. It follows that the cognitive resources necessary for responsible choice are acquired. The point is not that there is some particular set of cognitive skills that somehow defines the capacity for rational choice. The intellectual requirements for responsible choice will differ depending on the character of the issue. Nonetheless, the capacity for responsible choice depends on achieving a degree of intellectual sophistication. Education is a prerequisite of autonomy.

These observations have significant import for the view we must take of the rights of the student in the teacher–student relationship. They imply that *the teacher must see the student as more than a novice who is ignorant of the context and principles of the subject matter. The teacher must also see the student as a responsible moral agent who, because he is responsible for what he will believe and what he will do, must ask for and be given reasons for what he is asked to believe. He must also see the student as one whose capacity for understanding reasons must be expanded.*

Now this may seem paradoxical. I have, it would seem, argued both that the teacher has a moral duty to give reasons to the student and that the student is in no position to grasp these reasons. These claims are not, however, as inconsistent as might first appear to be the case. The argument I have given concerning the student's capacity to appreciate reasons shows that the student is not capable of viewing the subject matter from the perspective of the expert. This is a limit on the kinds of reasons a student can grasp concerning a subject, but it is far from showing that the student is altogether incapable of appreciating any reasons. The expert and the student will both approach any phenomenon with a set of concepts that they will use to assess the phenomenon or arguments concerning it. The concepts of the expert and the student will normally differ in scope and power, but the student does have a set of concepts that he can and will use to judge what he encounters in instruction.

These concepts are the students' court of appeal. They will provide the criteria by means of which the claims of a teacher will be judged and the context in terms of which these claims will be understood. The concepts of a given student may be more or less adequate to the instructional purposes of a teacher. A student, for example, who understands the atomic theory of matter is in a better position to understand the oxygen theory of combustion than one who does not. Students' concepts may also be dysfunctional. A student who sees matter as a continuous substance rather than as consisting of discrete parts cannot understand such phenomena as heat or the compression of gases, and the instructor will need to provide the student with reasons that suggest the inadequacies of this concept and the need for a different one.

We thus know two important things about the 'epistemic situation' of the student. We know that the student is not in the same position as the expert to assess the phenomena or the arguments of a discipline. We also know that the student has a position of his own from which the subject matter of a discipline will be assessed. Thus, the teacher cannot appeal to the student's epistemic situation as grounds for not giving the student reasons for what the student is asked to believe, although he may appeal to the student's epistemic situation as grounds for not giving the student the kinds of reasons that would be given to an expert. The teacher continues to have the duty to regard the student as a responsible moral agent, which entails the duty to give reasons within the student's capacity to grasp.

There is a second reason why the teacher has a duty to give the student reasons. The teacher has a duty to expand the capacity of the student for understanding and evaluating reasons. The giving of reasons is a necessary condition of a pedagogy that can expand this capacity. The meaning of the phrase 'giving reasons' should be broadly understood. It includes any device whereby a student can be made aware of the evidence for some claim. Verbal accounts of the reasoning for a claim are, no doubt, paradigmatic of giving reasons, but demonstrations, discussions, exercises or assignments that direct the student's attention to evidence are also included.

It is also to be insisted that reason-giving is an interaction between the teacher and the student that requires the student's active participation. Propositions that are objective evidence for some claim must be subjectively seen as evidence by the student. This requires the student to integrate reasons given by an instructor into the student's current concepts in such a way that they are structured as evidence within the student's cognitive structure. We must remember that a proposition or a phenomenon is only evidence for a claim in relation to a set of concepts that interpret it. The burning stick in our experiment is only evidence for the oxygen theory of combustion to the student with a proper set of prior assumptions. The suggestion that evidence is relative to the student's current concepts indicates a need on the part of the teacher to know what the student's current concepts are. There is, I think, no substitute for an active exchange between student and teacher in this regard. The clues to a student's concepts are the questions asked, observations proffered or counter-arguments produced. Reason-giving is thus not simply a process of transmission of ideas from teacher to student. It requires the participation of the student if it is going to succeed.

But reason-giving is far more than the way in which evidence is obtained by students. It is the way in which students come to understand what counts as evidence. It is thus the means whereby students come to internalize the concepts and criteria that are appropriate to thought in a given area. Reason-giving does this in at least two ways: it provides models and exemplars of what counts as a reason in a given area, and it provides practice in the use of relevant criteria and concepts.

To get a handle on the idea of an exemplar we may return to the combustion example and ask what its role in instruction is. One answer is that it is a way of providing the student with evidence for the oxygen theory of combustion. I have already suggested grounds for believing that this is not an altogether acceptable view. While it is the case that the student is being shown a phenomenon that can be interpreted as a piece of evidence for the oxygen theory of combustion, it is also the case that *as evidence* it is a remarkably weak piece, particularly from the student's point of view. The particular phenomena can be given a coherent interpretation within another theory, and the student is not in a position to assess the strength of the interpretation provided.

A more plausible view of the role of such demonstrations is that they are the means whereby students learn how the abstractions contained in the theories, formulae and concepts of a discipline are applied and manipulated. The concepts of a discipline come to have their meaning both in terms of how they are connected with one another and how they are attached to phenomena. A good exemplar exhibits both sorts of meaning. In such a way, the student can begin to get a feel for the criteria that govern the use of such concepts, not by having the criteria stated, but by seeing them employed. Students learn the syntax of scientific concepts much as they learn the syntax of their own language – by seeing it in use. Exemplars also perform the role of showing how the concepts and abstractions of a field attach to the phenomena with which they are concerned. This 'attachment' can involve several things. It can indicate the procedures by which abstract terms are given empirical meaning by showing how quantities are measured or experiments conducted. Simultaneously, an exemplar shows the student how to *see* a phenomenon through the concepts of a theory: the student is taught to see burning as oxidation. An exemplar may be part of the justification for some scientific theory, but its fundamental role in teaching is to allow the student to see the phenomenon in the way in which the expert can see it and in doing so to learn what counts as justification.

An exemplar need not be an empirical demonstration of the application of some scientific theory. What will count as an exemplar will depend on the problem or the field. It may be the analysis of a poem or painting, the diagnosis and treatment of a disease, or a paper that contains a classical treatment of a classical problem. The important thing is to exhibit the application of the concepts and techniques of a field to a representative problem.

The role of the instructor in transmitting the standards of a field is to be a model of competent performance. When a teacher gives the reasons for a given claim, he is giving the student a justification for it. But again, the point of the activity is not so much to justify the claim to the student, but to help the student to see what counts as a justification. The teacher does this by exhibiting the argument forms and criteria extant in a field in the process of giving reasons.

These ways of communicating or exhibiting the concepts and criteria of a field can be successful only when they elicit the active participation of the student. One reason is that the student's participation allows the instructor to see the student's view of the matter and to express a justification in a way appropriate to the student's current concepts. A second reason is that participation is a means of practising the intellectual skills of a field.

People do not learn an intellectual skill merely by watching it employed, any more than they learn a language merely by listening to others talk. Part of modelling is practice. The learner attempts an approximation of what he has seen. The teacher will respond in a way that highlights how the student's efforts fall short of the standard. Practice is an essential part of bringing any action into conformity with a standard. It is impossible unless the student is an active participant in the process of learning.

These arguments should suffice to show that reason-giving is both a moral and a pedagogical necessity for teaching. They also imply much concerning what the pedagogical relationship should be like and the kinds of freedoms that should and should not be available to students. These arguments indicate that *the pedagogical relationship should be governed by two fundamental ideas:*

(1)   there is a significant inequality between the student (as novice) and the teacher (as expert) in terms of their current capacity to understand and assess the ideas and arguments of a field;

(2)   the student and the teacher are equally moral agents and owe one another the rights and respect due moral agents.

The expertise of the teacher conveys certain kinds of authority upon the teacher over the student. The teacher's competence generates the right to govern the intellectually rooted decisions concerning teaching and learning – that is, decisions that require expertise in the concepts of a discipline to make them competently. Included in this category are the selection and organization of the curriculum, the right to direct the process in the classroom in profitable directions, and the right to evaluate the intellectual competence of the student's work. When admission to an intellectual profession is at issue this, too, is the prerogative of experts.

The teacher also owes certain duties to the student. Included are the obligations to represent the field to the student honestly and fairly, to evaluate the student's work on relevant criteria, to give reasons, and to initiate the student into standards of the discipline.

The student likewise has a set of rights and duties. The student has the right freely to inquire, to ask for reasons, to open access to information, and to question and debate the conclusions reached by experts. These 'intellectual liberties' secure for the student the right to participate in the intellectual affairs of the classroom in a way that assists the student in internalizing the standards and procedures of a discipline. And they recognize the student's status as a moral agent who is ultimately responsible for his beliefs and actions.

I have argued that the teacher has certain kinds of authority over the student. However, the student also has a *prima facie* right to be a voluntary participant in the pedagogical relationship. The grounds for this are again both moral and pedagogical. That the student is a responsible moral agent is grounds for making his participation in an educational situation voluntary.

From a pedagogical perspective, the point is that rational learning cannot but be voluntary. Students may be made to go to class and do homework. They cannot be made to internalize the standards and values of an intellectual enterprise. This kind of learning requires the willing involvement of the student in the enterprise.

Lest this emphasis on the voluntariness of the student's participation be misunderstood, let me note that this does not entail that there be no required courses, or required standards, or that academic decisions be made either democratically or in response to 'consumer demand'. There are academic decisions legitimately made by experts. The real issue is that students must accept the legitimacy of the education to which they are asked to submit. Education can take place when students believe that educational institutions are in possession of something worthwhile. Since the values and standards of intellectual enterprises are internal to these enterprises and cannot be fully appreciated by the novice, the student's submission to his education cannot be fully rational. It must be based, in part, on trust.

Education loses its legitimacy when students begin to believe that the values educators or educational institutions pursue are self-serving or perverse. They will then either drop out or come to see themselves as a captive audience. Genuine education ceases when students see themselves as held to their tasks by coercive factors, as, for example, when they see their economic future arbitrarily linked to some level of educational attainment. Students may go through the motions, pass the tests, and gain the certificates. A few may even be seduced into an appreciation of the forms of life intellectual enterprises represent. On the whole, however, when students lack a commitment to the value of what they learn, the consequences of learning on their values and their view of the world – the things that matter – will be minimal.

Demands for democracy or voluntariness in the detail of course selection, curriculum or instructor are signs that education is not seen as legitimate. The arguments I have given concerning the 'epistemic gap' between novice and expert indicate that yielding to such demands is not the cure for the disease of illegitimacy. Democracy in academic affairs is governance by the incompetent. An institution faced with such demands or with passive resistance to the education it provides needs, rather, to look to the values it pursues and how these values become viable to its students.

Some further caveats concerning the way in which education should be voluntary are required. I initially suggested that students have a *prima facie* right to be voluntary participants in the pedagogical relationship. That the right is *prima facie* suggests that there are considerations that may override it. There are two sorts of considerations. I shall note them here and take them up in more detail in later chapters.

The first is that a lack of maturity can override the right to voluntariness. General maturity must be distinguished from intellectual competence. The novice in physics lacks competence in the standards of physical argument. Such a person may, however, be mature. Maturity is the general capacity to discover or choose a stable and rational set of goals, needs and interests and make choices that further them. A student who does not know physics may, nevertheless, know himself well enough and know enough about what physics is like to make a competent (if tentative) commitment to study it. A student who lacks maturity cannot do even this. Some form of paternalism toward such a student's education may, therefore, be warranted.

Second, a student's choices may have an impact not only on himself, but on others. A student who fails to learn to read harms not only his own prospects, but those of others. In such cases, the society has some interest in the decision and may act coercively when a significant threat to its legitimate interest exists.

I assume that these restrictions on the voluntariness of student decisions apply primarily to younger children.

This view of the pedagogical relationship can best be summarized by calling it a master–apprentice relationship. *Its essential features are that the student is seen as a junior member of a community united by a shared commitment to some intellectual enterprise. Learning is a result of participation in the characteristic activities of the group under the guidance of an expert who sets educational tasks within the student's competence and evaluates performance. The relationship assumes the competence and the honesty of the master. Since the learner is not in a position to evaluate fully the competence of the master, the success of the relationship depends on trust. The learner in turn must willingly submit to the expertise of the master.*

When this master–apprentice relationship concerns some intellectual endeavour, I have suggested that the student has intellectual liberties that may appear quite similar to the intellectual liberties that are shared by members of intellectual communities and are exercised in the activity of inquiry. For the student, after all, learning is inquiry. The student thus has the right to relevant information and to question and debate the ideas he encounters.

It is, however, crucial to note that the student's intellectual liberty differs from that of the expert. Intellectual liberty for the expert is justified as an essential component of the institutional arrangements in which inquiry can be conducted and truth pursued. Intellectual liberty is the means whereby new ideas are subjected to the standards of the field and are accepted, rejected or modified. Intellectual liberty for the student, on the other hand, is a condition of the student exercising his responsibility as a moral agent and participating in an intellectual enterprise in a way likely to lead to the internalization of the concepts and standards of that enterprise.

Consider some features concerning these arguments. Note first that the appeal to moral agency is a non-consequentialist argument. It argues for granting intellectual liberty to students, not because doing so has beneficial consequences, but rather because doing so recognizes their status as moral agents. This moral argument for liberty does not, however, sharply distinguish the role of the expert from the role of the student, for the simple reason that the argument applies to any moral agent and therefore to novice and expert alike. Perhaps the only salient difference here is that there is more need to insist on the rights of students as moral agents since students are more likely to be in a subservient position than are experts.

The epistemological arguments for liberty distinguish more sharply between the expert and the novice. The student faces a task logically similar to that of an expert: new ideas must be assessed, and accepted, modified or rejected on the basis of relevant evidence. But the tasks are also different. For the expert the standards of the enterprise are known – the point of the inquiry is to add to human knowledge. The novice, however, has not internalized the standards of the enterprise – the point of inquiry is to do so. Moreover, while the student may be adding to his personal store of knowledge, he is not likely to add to the general store of human knowledge. That the student is a novice means that he is hardly in a position to do so. Arguments that justify liberty on grounds that it is a precondition of productive inquiry are not, therefore, likely to be successful when applied to students.

This difference in justification of intellectual liberty suggests that the nature of the particular liberties available to the expert and the student may differ as well. The major difference is that the intellectual liberties available to the novice are constrained by the requirements of effective pedagogy and may, therefore, be regulated by the teacher. The tenured professor or lecturer has earned the right to pursue his inquiries regardless of where the argument leads. Perhaps no one is required to publish his ideas or reward him for them, but neither is anyone empowered to stop his inquiry. The student, however, has not similarly earned the right to pursue his ideas or interests beyond the point where they contribute to his education or the education of his peers. The teacher thus has the right to curtail a line of inquiry when it becomes fruitless or disruptive. This does not mean that the teacher should cut short every line of thought that diverges from the truth – students learn from following a false trail. But it does mean that the teacher may cut short an unprofitable pursuit because he can see that it leads nowhere. The liberty of students has a different point from the liberty of the expert, functions according to a different set of rules, and can be regulated by the teacher. We shall need to give more detailed attention to precisely how the rules differ. That, however, is a task for a later chapter.

# CHAPTER 4

# The Social Application of the Epistemological Arguments for Liberty

We need to broaden the range of issues beyond the school. Epistemological arguments of the sort we have considered heretofore in the context of educational institutions and academic freedom have commonly been applied to the society at large. Free speech and a free press are defended by appeals to the claim that free and open discussion promotes competent and rational decision-making much as it promotes inquiry. Our inquiry on this point should suggest two important questions to ask about liberty at the social level.

First, the discussion of intellectual liberty has taken a decidedly elitist and anti-democratic turn. It has given a measure of authority to those who have mastered the central concepts of academic disciplines. We shall have to ask if these elitist arguments are to be applied to the society at large and if they are incompatible with democratic institutions.

Second, while epistemological arguments have been used to justify social liberty, they are by no means the only arguments that have been so employed. We shall have to discuss other arguments and determine the extent to which they apply to educational institutions.

I shall proceed here by examining the case for liberty made by John Stuart Mill in his essay 'On Liberty'. Mill's work is the classical defence of freedom of opinion and is also the paradigm case of the application of epistemological arguments to a social context.

Before we look at Mill's specific arguments for freedom of opinion, a few remarks on the larger philosophical context in which his arguments are embedded are required. Mill is quite explicit that he intends to give utilitarian arguments for his views; that is, his ultimate appeal is to the greatest good for the greatest number. In Mill's words:

> . . . I forego any advantage which could be derived to my argument from the idea of abstract right as a thing independent of utility. I regard utility as the ultimate appeal on all ethical questions.[1]

Mill's general strategy in defending liberty is to show that the varieties of liberty promote the general happiness. The major instance of this strategy is to show that liberty promotes the pursuit of truth, which in turn promotes competent and rational decision-making, which in turn promotes the general happiness. Despite the fact that the pursuit of truth is subordinate to happiness in Mill's scheme, it is the fact that Mill sees the pursuit of truth as a basic social value that largely determines the focus of his arguments. His basic question concerns the kinds of social arrangements that promote individual and collective inquiry.

Mill is also deeply concerned about what he sometimes refers to as the tyranny of the majority. He assumes the actuality and legitimacy of democratic authority, but he questions its limits. What are the limits on the right of a democratic majority to regulate the beliefs of individuals or minorities? Mill's response is the following:

> . . . the sole end for which mankind are warranted, individually or collectively, in interfering with the liberty of action of any of their members is self-protection. That the only purpose for which power can be rightfully exercised over any member of a civilized community, against his will, is to prevent harm to others. His own good, either physical or moral, is not a sufficient warrant . . . The only part of the conduct of anyone for which he is amenable to society is that which concerns others. In the part which merely concerns himself, his independence is, of right, absolute.[2]

For his more detailed defence of liberty Mill divides liberty into two sorts. He refers to the first as liberty of thought and discussion, and the second as individuality. We need here to be concerned only with liberty of thought and discussion. Mill provides an excellent summary of his arguments:

> First, if any opinion is compelled to silence, that opinion may, for ought we can certainly know, be true. To deny this is to assume our infallibility.
>
> Second, though the silenced opinion be an error, it may, and very commonly does contain a portion of truth; and since the general or prevailing opinion on any subject is rarely or never the whole truth, it is only by the collision of adverse opinions that the remainder of the truth has any chance of being supplied.
>
> Thirdly, even if the received opinion be not only true, but the whole truth, unless it is suffered to be, and actually is rigorously and earnestly contested, it will, by most of those who receive it, be held in the manner of a prejudice, with little comprehension or feeling of its rational grounds. And not only this, but fourthly, the meaning of the doctrine itself will be in danger of being lost or enfeebled, and deprived of its virtual effect on the character and conduct; the dogma becoming a mere formal profession, inefficacious for good, but cumbering the ground and preventing the growth of any real and heartfelt conviction from reason or personal experience.[3]

These arguments can be put in two groups. The first two arguments have to do with the social conditions of inquiry. They argue that any individual can be the source of new ideas and that truth is characteristically achieved as the result of a clash of ideas. The second two arguments have more to do with the comprehensibility and vitality of ideas than with their truth. Here Mill implicitly recognizes a significant epistemological point: the meaning of an idea is not something independent of its justification. To know what a claim actually says is to know what counts for and against it. Thus, when people fail to seek its justification, they begin as well to lose their grasp on what it means. Needless to say, when an idea loses its meaning it ceases to be a functioning guide to action. One cannot act on an idea one does not understand.

I have no quarrel with this second set of arguments. Indeed, I regard them as a variant on the theme argued in the previous chapter concerning the merits of participation for learning. These arguments, however, appeal to norms that are different from and less central to Mill's position than the first two arguments. In the second set of arguments Mill implicitly appeals to the notion that widespread understanding of ideas and their implications is socially desirable. No doubt it is. The real force of his argument, however, depends on the view that 'The truth of an opinion is part of its utility'. It is, thus, the first two arguments that are the foundation of liberty of thought and expression. They are the ones we must consider.

Mill was an empiricist. Indeed, he is one of the major figures among empiricist philosphers. His views on liberty of thought and discussion do not, however, fully reflect his empiricist commitments. Mill's empiricism is least reflected in the argument that truth emerges from the clash of ideas. I have already argued that empiricism does not provide a coherent account of the point of criticism and debate in inquiry. Mill's commitment to a 'marketplace of ideas' seems more an extension of his economics than of his epistemology. On the other hand, empiricism's commitment to fallibilism is clearly seen in Mill's claim that no one is entitled to be so certain of his views that he can confidently assume that in silencing others he is silencing error. Mill presumes that anyone can be the source of a new idea and that new ideas emerge from diversity of experience. Here the democratic character of empiricism is most clear: experience is the source of ideas; since everyone has experience, anyone can be the source of ideas.

Perhaps Mill's empiricism is also to be seen in his comments on the role of the clash of ideas. He does, at least, extend the right to participate in the marketplace of ideas to everyone. On the other hand, Mill often expresses the rather non-empiricist assumption that people differ in their competence to function in a marketplace of ideas and draws moderately elitist conclusions. Consider:

> The initiation of all wise or noble things comes and must come from individuals; generally, at first from some one individual. The honor and glory of the average man is that he is capable of following that initiative; that he can respond internally to wise and noble things, and be led to them with his eyes open . . . It does seem, however, that when the opinions of masses of merely average men are everywhere become or becoming the dominant power, the counterpoise and corrective to that tendency would be the more and more pronounced individuality of those who stand on the higher eminences of thought.[4]

Such remarks give a rather different perspective on Mill's views than what heretofore may have seemed to be the case. We no longer get a picture of truth being achieved from a kind of widespread intellectual free for all. It now appears as more of a professional sport when the vast majority of mankind have been relegated to the status of spectators. Most of us, it seems, can appreciate the sport of thinking, but few can play in the big leagues.

I wish to argue that this elitist turn to Mill's arguments is the natural expression of seeing liberty as a means to promote inquiry. Moreover, I suspect that it is only a kind of vestigial commitment to empiricism that keeps us from seeing the extent of the elitist implications of an appeal to the conditions that promote inquiry as the basic justification of liberty.

I have, of course, already argued something much like this. I wish, however, to augment those arguments for the authority of ideas with one additional argument, the point of which is to show that democracy is positively destructive of thought. Perhaps before doing so I should notify the reader that I shall not accept the anti-democratic implications of this argument. An inspection of the argument and its defects should, however, prove instructive.

My argument depends on the following claim. *Inquiry is not simply a matter of individuals collecting evidence to support or reject ideas. It is a social process. Among its requirements are coherent mechanisms whereby it can be decided what questions are to be answered, how they are to be answered, and when they have been answered. Such mechanisms will be found largely in groups of individuals who share common assumptions – a common paradigm, if you will. They are unlikely to occur in a coherent way in a mass pluralistic society.*

Consider a hypothetical case. Let us suppose we wish to discover a cure for the dread disease of chronic pulchritude. In order to do so we establish and equip a research facility and, being of an egalitarian bent, we staff our facility with a random sample of individuals drawn from the population of the city in which the facility was built. As it turns out, our staff consists of a philosopher, several physicians, an electrician, several business men, a few cashiers, a number of assorted skilled and unskilled labourers, a truck driver and a biologist. They begin with a meeting to decide how to approach the problem. A variety of approaches and issues is suggested. Several people argue that pulchritude is a social disorder, a product of monopoly capitalism. The businessmen vigorously disagree. The biologist argues that pulchritude is a hereditary disease and must be approached by isolating the gene that carries the disease and working out its DNA structure. The philosopher argues that the epistemological foundations of that claim are obscure and proposes to begin by clarifying them. The two physicians are persuaded by the biologist and urge acceptance of his views. Someone asks whether DNA is a sandwich and expresses the hope that Gene will bring him one, too. The group finds they cannot agree on an approach. They do agree, however, that everyone should begin work on the approach that seems best to him, and they agree to establish a weekly inter-office newsletter in which each person can report his progress to all of the others. They elect a publications committee to take care of the newsletter. The biologist (who happens to be correct) and the physicians decide to work on a common approach, but to do so independently, communicating with each other through the newsletter.

The publications committee runs into early problems. They receive more progress reports than they have space for. Moreover, they cannot agree on which reports really report progress. They decide to select those reports that can be understood by everyone on the staff, and they conscientiously poll the staff about which articles they found most enjoyable. No articles by the philosopher or the biologist are ever deemed well-written enough or of sufficiently general interest to be published. The two physicians and the biologist each assume that the others have made no progress, despite the fact that the biologist has turned up a promising lead. Moreover, one of the physicians knows a key fact that, if it was known to the biologist, would allow him to proceed rapidly.

At the end of two years of work the funding for the facility has run out. Several members of the staff believe they have made considerable progress, but no one is able to persuade anyone else of this. The group is unable to agree on an interim report. Funding is withdrawn and the project cancelled.

Could it have ended differently? Perhaps if they could have agreed on an approach at the outset it might have. They might at least have eliminated some wrong approaches or learned something by trying them. Had they got round to the biologist's view, pulchritude might have ceased to be the scourge of mankind.

The point: *communities of individuals who are trained in and united by a particular way of seeing and solving problems are essential to intellectual progress. They can focus on problems, generate approaches to them and identify progress. They can track down false leads and decide when they should be abandoned. Democratic bodies cannot do these things because they lack a locus of intellectual authority.* They can only be a tower of Babel. Democracy will prevent a coherent approach to problems. It will make it more difficult for those with a common approach to communicate unless, of course, they organize themselves into an intellectual community and cease to behave democratically. And when someone happens to triumph over these obstacles and finds something out, a democratic body will lack the means to certify that discovery. There will be no way for what an individual knows to become something that is known.

These problems can only be solved by varieties of elitism. People who share common commitments must unite to work out those commitments and exclude those who do not share them or cannot successfully employ them. Moreover, they must persuade outsiders to recognize them as the appropriate body to decide what is known in a given area. Intellectual progress requires the exclusion and submission of the uninitiated. At best intellectual progress requires the uninitiated to be intellectual spectators. To the extent that they participate in or gain power over an intellectual endeavour they will corrupt it. The epistemological arguments thus generate elitist views.

Consider what does and does not follow from this argument. Its major point is that *truth is not likely to be the product of an open-ended intellectual free for all among individuals of widely varying competence, training and viewpoints.* Inquiry requires criticism and the freedom to express new and unpopular ideas, but it also requires social structures that can focus the intellectual resources of a coherent intellectual tradition on problems, that can enforce agreed upon standards of intellectual competence, and that can achieve some consensus concerning when an issue has been decided. This is something intellectual professions often can do because they possess a common intellectual tradition and institutions that referee the work of the field. Such groups can function properly when they can act autonomously. They must, thus, be isolated from the noise and distraction of democratic debate and from the interference of democratic power.

*It does not follow that intellectual liberty is pointless or that the state should be entitled to enforce some favoured doctrine or ideology.* State enforcement of an ideology undermines thought, whether it be the inquiries of an intellectual profession or the unstructured chaos of a public debate. I intend no conclusion that would empower the state to determine any intellectual matter. Nonetheless, the primary point of application of freedom of thought and inquiry is to intellectual elites. It is the intellectual exchange among the competent that can be intellectually productive. It is difficult to see how a broad and democratic application of intellectual liberty can be justified as a social condition of competent inquiry. No doubt much of what Mill says is true. Anyone can be the source of a new idea. But people are more likely to have a good idea if they are trained in some conceptual heritage that allows them to experience the world in profitable ways. Moreover, having a good idea counts for little if there are not coherent intellectual forums in which it can be recognized and refined. Likewise, no doubt truth can emerge from the collision of adverse opinions, but it will not do so unless those who clash share enough of a common viewpoint to decide what counts as a persuasive argument and unless there is some mechanism to identify the outcome of the argument. Mill's arguments make excellent sense – when they are made as arguments for academic freedom. They are far weaker as arguments for a democratic marketplace of ideas.

I can see two arguments opposed to this view. The first is to attack the general applicability of the Kuhnian epistemology that underlies it. The second is to construct a defence of liberty that does not rely on epistemological arguments.

The first objection to this elitist rendering of Mill's arguments holds that the argument uncritically describes a situation that applies only in very special cases, and expands it to include all cases of inquiry. The case I have made against a democratic application of Mill's arguments may apply very well in physics or in many of the natural sciences, but it is hardly the case that it applies universally. No doubt it makes little sense to have a democratic debate on the merits of modern quark theory, but other kinds of debates – political debates, for example – can surely be conducted in a more democratic fashion. Moreover, when we are looking at the civic application of Mill's arguments, it is politics that should be our concern, not physics. After all, the central point of liberty is to allow a democratic society to deliberate on its affairs in a rational and competent fashion. That a democratic intellectual free for all is unlikely to be fruitful in physics is not a compelling difficulty if an intellectual free for all can be profitable in politics.

Perhaps, then, we should ask what it is about physics that makes it unique and inaccessible. How might physics differ from other areas of thought? Consider some possibilities. First, physics has a single paradigm. Physicists share what is largely a common view of the world. When they disagree, they disagree within a set of shared assumptions that allows them to know what they are disagreeing about and how to settle their disputes. Second, the concepts physicists have evolved and that comprise this common view of the world are complex and sophisticated. Their difficulty level is such that a lengthy training period is necessary before anyone can begin to participate in the debates of physicists. The consequence of these two factors is that physics is done by members of a single community, an international community, whose members share a common heritage of concepts from which most of us are excluded. Their deliberations are inevitably non-democratic.

Clearly few other areas of thought exhibit these properties to the degree that physics does. Much thought in psychology occurs within frameworks that are much like a paradigm. Such paradigms express coherent and sophisticated intellectual traditions. But there are several of them. Freudians share a common view of the world, as do behaviourists. But their views of the world differ sharply. Each perspective organizes its own intellectual enterprise and generates its own community. An area of thought may thus have what I shall call multiple paradigms, each of which is itself reasonably clear, internally consistent and agreed upon by its adherents. Behaviourists, like physicists, share a common world view. The agreed upon assumptions that make one a behaviourist are perhaps not so clear or agreed upon as those that make one a physicist, but neither are they hopelessly obscure.

It can also be the case that the concepts that define a given enterprise and that identify its adherents are less clear and less agreed upon than those that define behaviourism. Marxists and liberals, for example, have characteristic and differing strategies for analysing political events and institutions, which are rooted in differing beliefs about man and society. These differing perspectives structure political thought much as any paradigm structures thought. But they lack the 'tight' structure of many paradigms. One cannot formulate what it is to be a liberal with the precision that one can formulate what it is to be a behaviourist. Liberals have enough of an intellectual tradition and share enough of a common view that ordinarily one can distinguish liberals from Marxists or conservatives. But the boundaries of these commitments are vague. They shade into one another. People may think like liberals on some issues and like Marxists on others, and the communities they organize will be loosely organized and diverse. Most contemporary political parties will illustrate nicely. Being a Tory or a Republican makes one something distinguishable from a Democrat, or a Labour supporter, but it does not make one anything terribly precise.

Concepts, I have argued, are tools. Thought does not occur without them. But not all concepts are organized as they are in physics. Physics stands at one end of a continuum. Its concepts are linked into an orderly conceptual entity. From this point one moves to enterprises like psychology with multiple paradigms to enterprises like politics or education whose 'paradigms' are both multiple and diffuse. One may imagine at the end of this path a situation where whatever concepts are used for thinking have no systematic and recognized linkages to one another. While any given individual must employ some set to think with, there is no reason to suppose that any two individuals will share a common set other than by accident. At this end of this continuum intellectual communities cannot exist.

Paradigms and more loosely organized concepts may also differ in terms of their accessibility. The concepts of physics are difficult and are often concerned with specialized activities or interests. They are unlikely to be readily available to people except through formal instruction. By contrast, many of the concepts in terms of which political issues are discussed are not highly esoteric or complex. Moreover, such issues are commonly discussed in readily available public forums. In a functioning democratic society, they are part of the air one breathes. They can, thus, be learned informally.

We now have some reasons to believe that the concepts of politics are quite unlike those of physics in several noteworthy respects. The conceptual frameworks of politics are multiple and diffuse. They cannot, therefore, be the exclusive property of some intellectual guild. Moreover, they are accessible. One can encounter them in comprehensible form in public places. Does this mean that an intellectually fruitful democratic marketplace of ideas is possible for politics and for similar enterprises in a way in which it is not possible for physics?

The answer to this question is interestingly ambiguous. On the one hand, widespread public debates of political issues can be and sometimes are profitable ventures. They are even intellectually profitable. On the other hand, they are not intellectually profitable in the sense that seems intended by Mill's arguments. Mill seems to envisage the marketplace of ideas as producing intellectual progress: new ideas will be put forth, evaluated, refined and added to the store of human knowledge. This is the kind of happening that seems to me to be quite rare from public debates. The campaigns of the 1980 American presidential election provide excellent illustration of the effect of popular forums on intellectual endeavours. One of the candidates proposed a massive reduction in government expenditures. Among the purposes of this proposal were the revitalization of American industry and the transfer of various endeavours from public to private or from federal to local control. The proposal itself had been developed and expanded in several conservative journals by professional economists. It had received serious but quiet consideration by the US Congress. It was then injected into the campaign with the result that it was modified and qualified to make it palatable to groups with diverse interests and that it was debated by slogans and slurs. The effects of the public debate were precisely the opposite of those Mill predicts. The idea was not refined, evaluated, held up to the searching light of reason. It was subjected to the withering obfuscation of images and clichés.

It is not that popular debates do not change ideas, perhaps even in profitable directions. But change, even profitable change, is not the same as intellectual progress. Intellectual progress involves coming to know something, which in turn requires any change in ideas to be a result of a reasoned consideration of evidence. Changes in popular conceptions, however, often occur by a process more akin to natural selection than to rational assessment. Ideas, often proposed by elites, trickle down into public forums where the response is a function of the public mood, which in turn is a product of propaganda and of recent events.

Thus far the argument suggests that it is not crucial that many ideas are more accessible to the larger public than are the ideas of physics. The broadly democratic marketplace of ideas lacks the social mechanisms that allow debate to refine and improve ideas. I want to insist, however, that it serves other functions. Among the most important are that it provides a forum in which people can express their interests in matters of public concern and that it allows people to judge wherein their interests lie. These are, I believe, important intellectual functions, but they do not require that the marketplace of ideas be a means to intellectual progress. These points can be best examined by moving on to a different approach to the problem and by asking whether there are lines of defence of liberty that do not see liberty primarily as a means of promoting inquiry.

Let us return to an earlier theme: human beings are persons. They are ends in themselves and they are moral agents who are ultimately responsible for what they believe and what they choose. These views provide the foundation for a concept of liberty that is broader and more defensible than Mill's. Before proceeding, let us add another assumption: persons are equal. Here I do not intend to claim that people are equal in any empirical way such as intelligence, attractiveness or skill. Rather I claim that these characteristics are irrelevant to one's value as a person. Whatever fundamental rights everyone has as persons, they have equally.

What liberties do persons have? That persons are responsible moral agents implies that they must have the widest possible latitude to choose their own values, principles and actions. It follows that, where it is possible for people to choose privately, they have a right to choose without interference from government or society. Where choices are collective, people have a right to participate equally in those choices.

That people are ends in themselves implies that they must be treated as objects of value and respect, which includes treating people's wants, needs and interests as having *prima facie* validity. That a person wants something is itself a reason why he should have it. It is not a sufficient reason: wants conflict; not everyone can have what they want. But respecting people's wants does require that we grant them the right to pursue their wants. That they are equal, means that they must be granted an equal right to pursue their interests. When collective decisions are made, people have an equal right to have their interests taken seriously and to participate in collective decisions.

These ideas suggest that liberty has a number of functions that are not intimately linked to Mill's notion of a marketplace of ideas. Consider these:

(1) *Liberty provides for independent choice.* Liberty permits the freedom to select one's own beliefs and one's own values. Here it is primarily defensive. It protects the individual from encroachment by others and by society. This sort of liberty includes freedom of religion. It must also include the right to paticipate in the life of a group or culture whose members share one's values. Thus, it includes such rights as freedom of association and, more broadly, the right to a pluralist society. And it must include the right of free expression insofar as free expression is a necessary part of sharing and living one's values and beliefs. It would be an odd view of freedom of religion, for example, that failed to include the right to express one's beliefs and to participate in the life of a religious community. Ultimately, this sort of liberty promotes the right of self-ownership – the right to be the author of one's self, of one's values and fundamental convictions. To view people as responsible moral agents requires that we grant them this sort of self-determination.

(2) *Liberty provides for the right to participate in collective choice.* When a society must make a collective choice concerning some matter, individuals have an equal right to

participate in this choice. This right presumably includes such notions as 'one man, one vote', but for our purposes it must also include the freedom to express one's interests and to argue and assert one's views concerning any public matter. Here the point of free expression is not the collective pursuit of truth. It is the working out of a policy that gives due regard to everyone's legitimate interests. A society that believes that people are entitled to want what they want and that believes that everyone has an equal right to have their wants and interests considered will have to discover ways to formulate and adjudicate between interests. Part of this process must be freedom of expression. It is freedom of expression that allows people to put their needs and interests before the public forum so that they can be coherently deliberated about. This view of the point of free expression makes a good deal more sense of most political processes than does the marketplace of ideas. Elections, for example, are not some odd way of searching for some political truth. They are mechanisms wherein groups and individuals vie to express their interests. Candidates are not trying to express some potential political truth for public scrutiny. They are doing a kind of vector analysis of the interests they hear expressed. Other things beinq equal, the successful candidate is the one who proves capable of finding the most coherent resolution of the broadest range of expressed interests. Freedom of expression is thus a requirement of a political system that recognizes the *prima facie* legitimacy of the interests people have and their equal right to pursue them.

(3) *Liberty provides the opportunity for competent choice.* The previous two points suggest that a free society must provide both for the right to participate in collective decisions and the right of protection from encroachment by the society. Both kinds of liberty require freedom of thought and expression. These rights assign significant responsibility to the individual for directing his own life and put a premium on competent choice. Thus, any society that respects these rights must also recognize that individuals require the resources on which competent choice depends. A society that wishes to provide such resources will have to make available at least three things. First is a basic education. In a free society, individuals who have to choose their own values and beliefs will need the ability to

assess and evaluate information. This requires at a minimum that they be literate and that they acquire the psychological and intellectual capacities on which sound judgement depends. Otherwise they can be nothing more than victims of propaganda and ignorance. Second, such a society will have to make information freely available. Otherwise people will not know what options there are for them to choose among and will not know what kind of evidence counts for and against these options. Finally, such a society will have to provide for public forums in which both individual and public choices can be discussed and debated. Such public forums provide both an information disseminating and an educational function. The disputations of the members of a free society are a major way of discovering personal and collective options. Moreover, such disputations are often a way in which people can learn to be competent in understanding and assessing options. Public forums provide the opportunity for the individual to participate in the use of concepts that can be important to decisions. They can play the kind of educational role I have argued for participation. With respect to such concepts, which include those that concern values, moral principles and political judgements, it is crucial that they be accessible to everyone and not become the property of experts or of an elite. The importance of the public accessibility of such concepts is not that they make possible some sort of collective pursuit of truth, but that they provide at least the potential for a higher level of sophistication for individuals who face the moral imperative of being responsible for their own decisions and the necessity of pursuing their interests in public deliberations. That moral or political concepts are more accessible to the general public is thus an important fact after all, but it is important because it is a requirement of a free society that its most important concepts not become the property of experts. A free society can have its physics become the prerogative of an elite. The alternative is conceptual chaos. But its basic moral concepts must be publicly accessible. The alternative is moral fascism.

Where has this discussion led us? The first important conclusion is that we have placed the arguments for a free society on firmer foundations and on foundations that are suitably democratic and non-elitist. *Free institutions result from the recognition that human beings are free moral agents who must therefore be responsible for their choices.* Moreover, we can begin to get a sense of the source of the weakness of Mill's defence of liberty – its reliance on consequentialist arguments. The goal is to increase happiness, to maximize the average utility. Free institutions promote the average utility because they promote the pursuit of truth and 'The truth of an opinion is part of its utility'. But this argument founders on the shore of contemporary epistemology, which has indicated that inquiry is an activity that occurs most successfully in communities of experts united by shared intellectual commitments. Democracy is usually an obstacle to inquiry. It is rarely an asset. I have argued, however, that free institutions express the social requirements of moral agency. Intellectual liberty is required if people are to be responsible for their choices. If all people are to be responsible moral agents, then free institutions must be democratically available. Lest I be misunderstood, I wish to emphasize here that I am not claiming that truth is not important. Clearly, individuals who must choose responsibly will also want to choose wisely. They cannot be indifferent to the truth. *The real source of Mill's difficulty, then, is not his emphasis on the pursuit of truth, but his failure to insist that the imperatives of moral agency require this pursuit to be the concern and endeavour of every man.* Mill misses this point because his commitment to utilitarian precepts makes happiness, not moral agency, the central value. If it turns out that the average utility is best served by an elitist form of liberty, so be it. A genuine commitment to intellectual liberty is thus better served by attending to the Socratic maxim – the unexamined life is not worth living – than by attending to the utilitarian emphasis on the greatest good for the greatest number. Here perhaps we might better listen to a sentiment of Mill than harken to the detail of his official doctrine.

It is better to be a human being dissatisfied than a pig satisfied; better to be Socrates dissatisfied than a fool satisfied. And if the fool, or the pig, are of a different opinion, it is because they only know their own side of the question. The other party to the comparison knows both sides.[5]

Adequately liberated from its utilitarian framework, it is the correct thought.

We must also keep in mind, however, that some features of Mill's arguments make better sense in educational contexts. For certainly among the purposes of educational institutions are the promotion of inquiry and the dissemination of its results, research and teaching. Educational institutions must therefore be attentive to the conditions that promote inquiry and the initiation of the novice into available intellectual traditions. Moreover, the social conditions that promote competent research and teaching include elitist authority relations. Ideas and those who possess them have an appropriate degree of authority in educational institutions. At the same time, we must recognize that students are more than novice scholars; they are also moral agents with the duties and obligations of moral agents.

We have now transformed the paradox with which we began this discussion. *People are born free: as moral agents they have the duty to be the authors of their own thoughts. Yet people who would be competent thinkers must commit themselves to mastery of the tools, and this requires submission to a conceptual heritage.* When applied to the authority structure of educational institutions this paradox resolves itself into the following features:

(1) *The justification of academic freedom is significantly different from the justification of intellectual liberty in the larger society.* While each justification involves the pursuit of truth, academic freedom is primarily concerned with the social conditions that maximize effective research and teaching. Liberty outside an academic setting, however, is primarily concerned with the conditions of responsible choice.

(2) *Arguments for academic freedom are elitist in character in that they indicate that the free exchange of ideas is an enterprise likely to promote the advancement of human knowledge when it is engaged in by experts.* The student as novice, however, has a duty to submit to the authority of ideas and the authority of those who possess them. Liberty outside an academic context must be democratically available, because it seeks to promote the widest possible oppor-

tunity for competent and responsible choice.

(3) *Actual educational practice must find a balance between these perspectives on intellectual liberty.* Teachers do not cease to be moral agents when they become experts, nor do students cease to be moral agents because they are novices.

(4) *Educational institutions are also social institutions.* They too must ultimately be responsive to the demands of moral agency. And other social institutions have an educational role. They too must be responsive to the requirements of intellectual competence.

The result of these arguments is that we have two perspectives on intellectual liberty. The task is not to choose between them, but to balance them in rational ways. Educational authority must reflect an effective integration of the requirements of intellectual competence and the requirements of moral agency. We have already briefly discussed the character of this integration in the context of the pedagogical relationship. The larger task, to express the integration in the authority structure and governance of diverse educational institutions, still lies ahead.

# II

# Liberty and Educational
# Institutions

# CHAPTER 5

# Academic Freedom

*Freedom to express and to publish unpopular ideas is essential to inquiry and to the growth of knowledge.* I have expressed some doubt about this doctrine as a defence of freedom of thought and action as broadly based civil rights. There are other, more persuasive arguments for liberty. But as an argument for academic freedom it is persuasive. Criticism is essential to inquiry. Any society that wishes to promote inquiry and advance knowledge must, therefore, find effective ways to institutionalize criticism.

It will be helpful in seeing the point of academic freedom to start with a statement of an opposing view.

> To begin with, no institution, based upon the philosophical presuppositions of its founders and directors, can achieve total neutrality. But not only is total neutrality unachievable, it is also undesirable, especially if the university in question is tax-supported. When citizens . . . have a portion of their income confiscated for purposes of educating other citizens . . . they should at least be offered the minimal assurance that their tax dollars will be used to train loyal citizens and not revolutionaries.[1]

This passage represents a paradigm case of the view that the notion of academic freedom was designed to oppose. Academic freedom is intended to permit scholars to follow their thoughts where they lead and to advocate unpopular ideas when it seems to them that there are reasons to do so. The standard case of violation of academic freedom is when a faculty member is punished or his contract terminated because he has taken a position that is at odds with the views of those who pay the bills or who wield power.

Thus, the fundamental requirement of academic freedom is the protection of the privileges and security of those who hold unpopular views from those inside or outside the university who hold power. Institutions committed to the advancement of human knowledge must, therefore, take the view that those who pay the bills are not, as a consequence, entitled to a say about what views may and may not be held by those scholars whose salary they pay. That an institution is publicly financed does not give politicians, boards of trustees or legislators the right to dictate the institution's ideology.

The passage also indicates that a second requirement of academic freedom is institutional neutrality. If individual scholars are to have the freedom to inquire, an institution cannot have an official point of view. When an institution *per se* has an opinion, the capacity of the members of that institution to assess that opinion critically is at best inhibited and at worst prohibited. It is, of course, appropriate for a church or a political party to have opinions that its members may be expected to share. Such groups exist to express or promote a point of view. But a university exists to advance knowledge and learning. If it is to do so, its members must be free to pursue their ideas where they lead. A university that is Catholic or Protestant, conservative or communist, in any way that binds the views of its members, cannot be fully a place where truth is sought.

This rather standard account of academic freedom is not, however, sufficient, for as yet it contains no account of academic authority. Universities and other intellectual communities do and must make decisions about people and about their work. Not everyone who wants to be a professor can be. Not everyone who is hired by a university can be kept on. Not every paper that is written for publication can be published. How are academic communities to decide who is to be hired, promoted or published in ways consistent with the values of free inquiry?

There are two rules that are generally laid down as part of an account of a system of institutional authority that is supposed to be consistent with academic freedom. The first rule is that *such academic decisions as are made about people or their work are to be made on grounds pertaining to the competence of the person or his work, but may not be made on grounds of whether one agrees with his opinions or conclusions.* Intellectual enterprises have standards. How closely a person's work conforms to the standards of competence in his field is the central question in judging him or his work. Moreover, the quality of a person's work is a matter that can be determined independently of the conclusions reached. Judging competence is normally a matter of judging the quality of the arguments given, rather than deciding whether one likes the conclusions of those arguments.

The second rule follows from the first. *Individuals or their work must be evaluated by people who are in a position to judge the competence of their work.* This means that academic evaluations will first and foremost be made by a scholar's peers or by an elite among a scholar's peers. The presumptions are that it is the members of an individual's professional community who are in a position to know what a field's standards are and that it is those among this group who have demonstrated a capacity for quality work who are apt to be the best judges.

The conclusion that follows from these considerations is that the *kind of authority that is consistent with academic freedom is the authority of referees; that is, the authority of experts brought to bear on the competence, but not the conclusions, of a person's work.*

Academic freedom thus requires a set of institutions that promote the following principle: *Scholars may not be rewarded, denied rewards or punished on account of the content of the views they express, but may be rewarded, denied awards or punished on account of the competence with which they argue their views.*

The discussion thus far points to at least three kinds of conditions that must be met if this principle is to be satisfied:

(1) Institutions are required that provide reasonable security for those who may wish to express an unpopular opinion.
(2) Educational institutions must not be committed to any particular doctrine. They must be neutral.
(3) Authority must be the authority of experts. Only a

scholar's peer group, particularly its most esteemed members, is entitled to exercise judgement concerning a scholar's competence.

Perhaps the paradigmatic expression of these ideas is the institution of tenure, whereby university professors and lecturers, after a probationary period and after having been judged competent by their peers, are given virtually an unbreakable lifetime guarantee of employment. In many parts of the world, tenure is the major defence of academic freedom.

I believe the doctrine of academic freedom I have sketched above to be generally correct and defensible. I also believe, however, that there are certain kinds of situations, I shall call them 'hard cases', where it is difficult to see how it can be coherently applied. I shall devote most of this chapter to these hard cases. In order to focus the issue, I would like to sketch three fictional cases, two of which are 'hard cases'.

(1) Professor Donald Dete is a professor of agricultural economics at the University of South Weeds. During the first years of his career he did a classical study on the marketing of cranberries that revolutionized the cranberry distribution system of South Weeds, significantly aided the economic development of the region, and earned Professor Dete the respect of his colleagues and a tenured chair at South Weeds.

Lately, however, Professor Dete has been looking at the system of agricultural labour in the cranberry business. He has begun to believe that cranberry pickers are greatly oppressed by large corporations who have bought up the cranberry bogs. Moreover, in order to develop a theoretical analysis for his views, he has become much interested in current Marxist views on agricultural labour. His most recent paper, 'Marxism in the Bogs', which expressed his new views, created a storm of protest. The regional chapter of the Bureau of Growers (BOG) held several meetings on the topic. As a result of these meetings BOG's president has informed the dean of Professor Dete's college of BOG's displeasure at Dete's work and has intimated that several grants funded by BOG are no longer certain. Moreover, a legislator from the cranberry district has let the president of South Weeds know that Professor Dete's work could be a factor in next year's appropriation for South Weeds. Professor Dete has been informed by his dean that it would be in everyone's best interest if he would turn his efforts in other directions.

(2) Professor DeGruve was a non-tenured faculty member at Innovation City Teachers College. His responsibilities were to teach urban studies and educational sociology to future teachers. Innovation City has recently revised all its teacher education programmes on the assumption that children are natural learners and that failure to learn must be a consequence of having been psychologically damaged by parents or improperly trained teachers. Teachers are, therefore, to be trained primarily in the diagnosis and treatment of neuroses. Part of the new programme, entitled Clinically Based Teacher Education (CBTE), requires each instructor to provide a list of clinical objectives (COs). These are statements of the particular diagnostic techniques and their cures that each course is intended to achieve. When asked for his list of COs, Professor DeGruve responded with a short paper arguing that CBTE was absurd and that he had no intention of reorganizing his courses to comply with the mandate. He subsequently wrote several papers on the topic and became something of a leader of the opposition to CBTE. The director of Innovation City Teachers College responded to Professor DeGruve in a letter, informing him that since Innovation City believes in academic freedom Professor DeGruve would not be forced to comply with the CBTE mandate, but that his courses would no longer be counted as part of the professional sequence for teacher certification. As a consequence, Professor DeGruve's course enrolments fell sharply. Moreover, since CBTE had become a national fad, Professor DeGruve, who was now considered behind the times, could not get funding to continue his research into teacher education. When the time came for his contract to be renewed, Professor DeGruve was let go. His writing on CBTE was cited positively as indicative of his intellectual competence, but his low course enrolments and his failure to do research on teacher education were regarded as major shortcomings. One passage from the report recommending his termination read, 'The central point is that Professor DeGruve

is not contributing to the mission of Innovation City Teachers College and is not doing the job for which he is paid. Were we to keep him on, we would have to hire someone else to do the job for which we hired him. Professor DeGruve is a competent teacher and scholar, but he does not fit into our programme and should be encouraged to find employment elsewhere.'

(3) Professor Sater teaches courses in phenomenology and existentialism in the Arts College of Stationary University. He was hired by a faculty consisting of philosophers trained in Anglo-American analytic philosophy who believed that it was desirable to acquaint philosophy students with philosophical traditions other than the dominant one. Professor Sater had been adequate as an instructor and had published successfully in several journals devoted to phenomenology and existentialism. The philosophy faculty of Stationary University was, however, unanimous in recommending against a promotion for Professor Sater. Part of their report read: 'Professor Sater appears to have had his writing published and appears to have secured some acceptance for it among those who read the journals in which it was published. We, however, are agreed that Professor Sater's writing meets no recognized standards of philosophical competence. It is dominated by the use of unclear and unanalysed language. Indeed, it appears devoted to the creation of a large barrage of hyphenated obscurity. What one is to make of phrases such as "Dasein-with" and "potentiality-for-being-as-a-whole" is beyond us. We understand neither the meaning of the terms nor the point of the question they are supposed to aid in addressing. The perpetuation of this plague of obscurity should not be rewarded because others with a similar disease profess to understand it.'

These three cases represent three rather different kinds of issues. The first is the typical case of academic freedom. Professor Dete has offended some power external to the university by taking a radical position opposed to its interest. Those offended by Professor Dete's work have put pressure on Professor Dete's institution to keep him in line, and the institution has done so. I shall treat the application of the doctrine of academic freedom to this case as non-controversial. Professor Dete's right to academic freedom has been violated. An institution that believes in academic freedom has a duty to defend Professor Dete's right to pursue his research and to publish his results.

The other two cases are hard cases. We thus need to distinguish them from the first case. Consider, then, the grounds that can be given for and against the claim that Professor DeGruve's right to academic freedom was violated. Professor DeGruve might argue that his academic freedom was violated in that the root cause of his dismissal was his opposition to CBTE. His failure to function in the teacher training programme and his failure to get his research funded were not consequences of his ineptness as a teacher or his incompetence as researcher. His abilities in these areas were adequately documented. His failures were directly traceable to his opposition to CBTE and his refusal to cooperate in a CBTE programme. When his institution decided to fire him, it, in essence, decided to punish him for his views.

Professor DeGruve might also argue that in establishing CBTE as its 'official' view of teacher certification, Innovation City Teachers College violated the doctrine of university neutrality. The institution has made a commitment to a particular view of teacher education that not even the institution believes to be uncontroversial. Moreover, it behaves with respect to this commitment in such a way as to make it virtually obligatory for the faculty. Those who do not agree with it cannot keep their jobs.

Finally, Professor DeGruve might argue that Innovation City Teachers College has effectively eliminated any possibility of a critical assessment of CBTE both by making faculty appointments in such a way that only those who accept CBTE are hired or retained and by linking institutional incentives, such as research grants, to agreement with CBTE. The diversity of the faculty is, thus, effectively eliminated so far as CBTE is concerned. CBTE maintains its standing among Innovation City Teachers College faculty, not by virtue of persuasion, but because faculty are selected because they agree with it and because their loyalty is maintained by the system of institutional rewards. Professor DeGruve can thus make a case that his right to academic freedom has been violated.

Innovation City Teachers College, however, does have some

counters to these arguments. Most importantly, it might insist that the institution has a mission that goes beyond teaching and research about education. Its central mission is to train teachers. While teaching and research about education are enterprises that can be competently conducted in the absence of any collective agreement concerning substantive educational issues, that is not true of teacher training. If an institution is to train teachers, it must have some view about how this is to be done. That requires some collective agreement on the basic direction and character of the enterprise. A decision not to have any collective view about the nature of the programme is a decision not to have a programme.

Innovation City might also argue that Professor DeGruve was not let go because he disagreed with CBTE. In fact, his articles against CBTE were counted in his favour. He was let go because of his refusal to cooperate with the CBTE programme. Any member of the faculty of Innovation City is free to hold and advocate any view about CBTE he wishes. Indeed, such criticism is highly valued, since it can only lead to a more reflective and, therefore, stronger programme. Thus, it is untrue that diversity and dissent are not tolerated at Innovation City Teachers College. The faculty, Professor DeGruve included, are free to hold and advocate any views that seem to them to be reasonable.

What are the issues? I trust it will be obvious enough to the reader that Innovation City Teachers College's claim that Professor DeGruve is actually free to hold whatever views he wants is spurious. It assumes that people for whom integrity and concern are important professional characteristics can simultaneously be expected regularly to behave in ways at odds with their professional convictions. One would not want a faculty capable of digesting the degree of hypocrisy required. Moreover, it assumes that people can succeed in implementing a view in which they do not believe, and it assumes that it is possible for an institution consistently to reward people for compliance with the behavioural requirements of a viewpoint while applying no coercion concerning their acceptance of this viewpoint. Such assumptions are absurd. Certainly, Innovation City has made acceptance of CBTE a condition of employment.

The real issue is whether they are entitled to do so, which

raises profound questions concerning what is meant by institutional neutrality. It is possible to interpret neutrality so narrowly that very much of what commonly goes on in contemporary universities would be prohibited. Professional schools would be prohibited insofar as they require some agreement on the part of their faculties concerning what counts as a competent professional and how competent professionals are to be trained. Moreover, it would be difficult to do research on specific social concerns or that required a degree of collective effort by a team of researchers. Cornell University, at which I work, has the world's foremost College of Agriculture. In addition, it has an extensive commitment to research in high energy physics. The College of Agriculture is devoted primarily not to the disinterested pursuit of truth about plants and animals but to teaching and research that promote the interests of agriculture in New York State. This commitment can substantially influence the kinds of research that are encouraged or discouraged. Research in high energy physics is a group enterprise. A colleague in physics recently noted being partly responsible for an article with 65 co-authors. The list of authors comprised 25 per cent of the article's text. The members of the team were hired to do very specific jobs. In both cases, people are hired to research particular problems or to fulfil a certain role on a research team. Their freedom to follow a question where it leads when that leads away from the institutional mission or away from one's role in a research team is often restricted.

Does neutrality prohibit mission-oriented teaching or research? If it does, the university's capacity to respond to particular social needs or to do collective research will be much inhibited. At the same time, if it does not, individual faculty members can be made subservient to the institution's sense of mission, much as Professor DeGruve became subservient to Innovation City Teachers College's commitment to CBTE. Here there is a significant conflict of worthy ends.

A second problem for academic freedom arises from mission-oriented enterprises. This is the problem of external control. When a university accepts the responsibility to accomplish some specific social mission, it must simultaneously accept the fact that the governance of such missions is not legitimately the sole responsibility of the university. If a university wishes only to study and teach about education, it can, perhaps, make a plausible defence of the proposition that it should have exclusive control over how that is to be done. The questions to be answered in making decisions about such teaching and research will be questions within the expertise of scholars of education. It is they who should decide. There is no compelling reason to consider the interest of those external to the university. However, once the university accepts the responsibility to train teachers, or once it accepts the responsibility to do research generated not by the concerns of the discipline of education but by the needs of the practice of education, it must also accept the fact that people external to the university have a legitimate and substantial concern for what the university does. Given this, it is perfectly reasonable for legislators, or whoever represents the interests of the public in education, to set the standards for the training and certification of teachers, and it is reasonable to expect educational institutions that train teachers to conform to these standards.

Mission-oriented universities thus legitimate external loci of control of their programmes. How can this become a problem for academic freedom? The general answer is that scholars may become subservient not only to the mission of their institution but also to the external authority responsible to oversee the mission. This violates the principle of peer judgement. Scholars may come to be judged not only on the basis of the competence of their work but on the basis of its perceived utility, and they may be judged not only by their peers, but by those whose interests they are expected to serve. For example, a professor of educational administration is likely to be evaluated by other scholars concerned with educational administration who will look primarily at the quality of his research. He is also likely to be judged by practising administrators who can be expected to exhibit little interest in the intellectual quality of his work but great interest in its utility.

Being subservient to a mission and to external control can alter the standards used to judge a scholar in ways ranging from rather heavy-handed and overt to quite subtle. External agencies may seek to dictate the conclusions of a scholar's research. Such occurrences seem not infrequent in mission-oriented institutions. Indeed, academics often engage in a kind of self-censorship for fear of offending those external to their institution whom they perceive as their clients. More subtly, the questions asked are likely to differ depending on whether they emerge from academic theory or from the area of practice. For example, given a question about school discipline, a philosopher or a lawyer is likely to transform it into a question of legitimate authority. Issues of rights and duties will emerge as central, since these are the concepts philosophers and lawyers use to discuss authority. Teachers are likely to find such debates substantially beside the point. Their concern is apt to be not so much with what they are entitled to do, but with what will be effective in controlling a class. Likewise, governmental agencies who sponsor educational research commonly complain that researchers who are asked to research a problem transform it from a problem that is germane to educational practice to one that is of interest to an academic discipline.

I suspect that most readers will agree that academic freedom should protect scholars whose research results prove objectionable to those whose interests the researcher is supposed to serve. That a scholar is supposed to engage in teaching or research that is useful to some group external to the university does not entitle that group to stipulate the truth. It is far less obvious, however, that those whom a university seeks to serve ought not to have something to say about the kind of research scholars engage in or the form the questions addressed take. Does a scholar whose position exists to do research that improves educational practice have a right to transform a question about effective discipline into one about legitimate authority when that is not what the teacher wishes to know? Here the issue is complex. It may be that the scholar is correct. Perhaps the right question is one about legitimate authority, or perhaps it is necessary to translate the question into the concepts of an academic discipline in order to investigate it at all. But who is right is only part of the issue. The more important part is the extent to which a scholar should have autonomy over a line of research that is intended primarily to improve practice in a given area rather than to answer the questions of academic theory. There is surely much plausibility to the suggestion that the clients of a researcher are entitled to some say about the nature of the research done. If this is true, it follows that a scholar's clients, as well as his peers, are entitled to an opinion concerning the merits of his work. Peer judgement cannot be the only legitimate form of evaluation in the mission-oriented institution.

We now have some sense of the parameters of our first hard case. *Academic freedom seems to require institutional neutrality and the peer evaluation of scholars. Mission-oriented institutions can erode each of these requirements. Having a mission requires an institution to have a view about what is socially desirable; it can legitimate the evaluation of scholars in terms of their commitment to the mission and legitimate people other than a scholar's peers having an opinion, at least on the utility of a scholar's work.*

If we are going to answer these questions, we shall have to take a more detailed look at the idea of neutrality itself and at the particular ways in which universities are supposed to be neutral. I shall proceed here by looking at some common objections to the view that universities should be neutral.

The first objection is that it is impossible to be neutral. The second is that neutrality is undesirable. Linked together, these objections often give a powerful argument to those who see the university as essentially a conservative institution serving those with power and opposing progressive social movements. The ideal of neutrality on this view will be seen not as a social condition of inquiry, but as a smokescreen behind which the university hides while in fact serving the interests of society's rich and powerful. Since the university cannot be neutral, it must serve someone's interests. Its only acceptable course, therefore, is to choose to serve the progressive elements of society. Since the university cannot act neutrally, it must act correctly.

Is it possible for a university to be neutral? Those who have wanted to say 'no' to this question have given two different kinds of arguments to support their contention. Often they point out various facts that suggest the difficulty of neutrality. They will, for example, point out the various forces that compel universities to take sides or that subtly structure the perceptions of the members of universities so that they implicitly take sides. A second argument maintains that neutrality is not only factually difficult, but logically impossible. Consider an argument by Robert Paul Wolff:

> As a prescription for institutional behavior, the doctrine of value neutrality suffers from the worst disability which can afflict a norm: what it prescribes is not wrong, it is impossible. A large university in contemporary America cannot adopt a value-neutral stance, either externally or internally, no matter how hard it tries ... One of the first truths enunciated in introductory ethics courses is that the failure to do something is as much an act as the doing of it. It is perfectly reasonable to hold a man responsible for not paying his taxes, for not exercising due care and caution in driving, for not helping a fellow man in need. In public life, when a man who has power refrains from using it, we all agree that he has acted politically ... acquiescence in governmental acts, under the guise of impartiality actually strengthens the established forces and makes successful opposition all the harder.[2]

These arguments, perhaps, have their point. However, they are not compelling in the form they are stated. Let us grant for the sake of argument that it is clear that it is factually impossible for a university ever to be completely and entirely neutral. Unfortunately, nothing of interest follows from this. It is a general characteristic of moral and political ideals that they are rarely fully achieved or achievable. It follows neither that we ought not to pursue them, nor that we cannot make considerable progress in pursuing them. No person is ever fully moral. No society is ever fully just. This hardly means that morality and justice cannot or should not be pursued. People can be made to be more moral. Societies can be made more just.

The claim that neutrality is logically impossible, if true, has more serious consequences. A situation is logically impossible when the conditions for its realization are incompatible. A round square is logically impossible. It must both have and not have corners. Such a situation is not only impossible, it cannot coherently be pursued. The degree to which something is round is the degree to which it is not square. Thus, if neutrality is logically impossible, it cannot serve as an ideal or a goal of action. Not only could we never fully attain it, we could not even pursue it.

But Wolff's argument cannot be correct, for it shows far too much. There are cases where failing to act is an act. If I see someone in danger and I can save him, then I have acted whether I do or do not try to save him. But this cannot be true of any act. For any conceivable act, *A*, it must be true that I am either doing *A* or I am not doing *A*. But not doing *A* cannot be the same as doing the action of not doing *A*. If 'not doing *A*' is the same as 'not *A*-ing', it follows that I am currently engaged in doing an infinite number of actions. I am doing the act of not doing everything there is to be done (except the act of not writing on a yellow pad). This passage is being written during a war between Iraq and Iran. By Wolff's logic, I am a double agent. I am busily helping Iran by doing the act of not helping Iraq, and I am busily helping Iraq by doing the act of not helping Iran. Not only that, but I am busily engaged in the doing of not doing a large number of other things, most of which I am not aware of. And I can even do all of these not doings while asleep. Either I am truly a remarkable fellow or something is wrong with Wolff's argument. While I have always thought myself truly remarkable, I have to confess that here the better conclusion is that something is wrong with Wolff's argument.

The general answer must be that not doing something is usually not an action. Wolff's claims must apply only under special conditions, which he has failed to specify. If we are to make further progress we need to know what the conditions are that make not doing *A* into not *A*-ing.

We have thus far found the arguments against the possibility of neutrality inconclusive. Certainly they do not make a compelling case against neutrality. Yet, they do suggest that neutrality might be difficult or impossible under some conditions. Perhaps there are cases where neutrality is so difficult that we cannot do any better no matter how hard we try. Or perhaps these are cases where not doing *A* is doing not *A*. To inquire further, therefore, it will be helpful to note some different kinds of neutrality to see if any of them are problematic in the above ways.

(1) *Neutrality of Consequences* (Nc): here the concern is for the consequences of an action. For some issue, *I*, an action, *A*, is neutral for *I* when neither doing *A* nor not doing *A* has consequences for *I*. Tonight I shall either have a bowl of popcorn or not. Since neither having the popcorn nor not having it will

have an impact on the nuclear arms race, the action is neutral $_c$ for the arms race.

(2) *Neutrality of Position* (Np): here neutrality is a matter of not having a view or a position about some issue. It is not taking a stand. Having a position often involves more than simply having a belief. (Indeed, one can have a position in which one does not believe.) It involves a degree of commitment. Thus, a person (or an institution) is neutral $_p$ with respect to some belief or some policy when he has not taken on a commitment to that belief or policy.

Neither of these kinds of neutrality is precisely what is required. Neutrality in the university is supposed to promote the process of inquiry and the growth of knowledge. This requires a view of neutrality that is active with respect to the university's intellectual functions. The university must not act or take positions that prevent its members from pursuing an argument where it leads or that inhibit criticism and debate. At the same time, the university must be able to promote and support the values and conditions that render inquiry effective. The kind of neutrality expected of a university is analogous to the kind of neutrality expected of a referee of a sporting event. Just as a referee must be impartial between the opponents in the game, a university must be impartial between intellectual combatants. This sort of impartiality does not, however, preclude the referee from making those judgements about participants required by the rules of the game. Nor does it require the referee to be neutral about the point of the game. Likewise, the sort of neutrality expected of a university does not preclude the university from making judgements concerning the competence of its members or from acting to promote its intellectual values. The kind of neutrality expected of a university is impartiality.

(3) *Impartial Neutrality* (Ni): impartial neutrality requires the university to act so as to support and promote the values and conditions of inquiry, while at the same time not taking a stand concerning the particular set of ideas currently under deliberation. The requirements of impartial neutrality can be made clearer by stating them as a set of rules as follows:

(a) *A university may have and may enforce no policy about the views that may be held or advocated by its members.* This is the basic condition. It is a case of neutrality of position. But it is not neutrality $p$ about everything. The object of neutrality is specified as the views of members of the university community.

(b) *A university may have no position or enforce no policy that has consequences for the views that may be held or advocated by its members.* This is a case of neutrality of consequences. Its point is to insist that a university may not justify actions that have the consequences of undermining the processes of free and open inquiry by claiming that this was only the consequence, but not the point, of its action.

(c) *A university may have positions and enforce policies favouring 'the epistemological virtues'.* Free inquiry has a point. It is supposed to promote the growth of knowledge. It would be absurd to adopt a view of neutrality that prevented a university from subscribing to those values that give meaning to the growth of knowledge. These values I have dubbed 'the epistemological virtues'. They include respect for truth, beauty, honesty, fairness, excellence and competence. A university is entitled to advocate them and to enforce policies that promote them.

(d) *A university is entitled to provide the support necessary to maintain its legitimate functions and may adopt the policies necessary to permit it to do so.* Universities do numerous things that are not themselves educational activities but that are required if educational activities are to take place. They operate dining halls and dormitories. They build buildings and mow lawns. They are entitled to have positions and policies about how these support services are performed.

These rules capture what is required by impartial neutrality. Is this an adequate view of what is required by university neutrality? We can test it by reconsidering two previous issues in its light and by raising one more problem.

What shall we say to those who claim that neutrality is neither possible nor desirable? The most obvious reply is that the concept of impartial neutrality is both possible and desirable. Some of the conditions may be difficult to achieve, but none is logically impossible. Moreover, this notion of neutrality is required if the central intellectual functions of the university are to be achieved. Its value makes neutrality worth pursuing in the face of significant obstacles.

It will, however, be illuminating to consider the claim that neutrality is neither possible nor desirable in more detail. Let us imagine a university asked to deal with some very pressing social issue, *I*. Consider, then, some arguments designed to show that a university cannot or should not be neutral about *I*.

One such argument consists in taking any lack of commitment to some view about *I* as opposition to that view. This strategy is captured in such phrases as 'If you're not part of the solution, you're part of the problem' and 'He that is not for me is against me'. I shall call this strategy the Zealot's Ploy. If failure to support a cause is to oppose it, then neutrality is logically impossible. The Zealot's Ploy is a variant of Wolff's argument that the failure to act is to act – *A* or not-*A*. Thus, the Zealot's Ploy is successfully refuted by the response to Wolff's argument. The Zealot's Ploy shows too much. It is capable of showing that a person is simultaneously on both sides of an issue, even if he is entirely unaware of the issue. This, however, is not a sufficient response, for there may be cases where an argument very much like the Zealot's Ploy makes quite good sense.

Suppose issue *I* concerns how a university is to invest its endowment. Suppose, for example, that the university of North Weeds is found to have invested a considerable sum in Repression Importers, Ltd. Repression Importers is a major importer of agricultural produce that has a widely deserved reputation for exploiting agricultural labour in developing countries. Having discovered North Weeds' investment in this notorious corporation, a committee of concerned faculty accuses North Weeds of employing its funds in a manner that supports inhumane labour practices and advocates that North Weeds withdraw its funds from Repression Importers. North Weeds makes the following response: North Weeds is entitled to and, indeed, has an obligation to use its financial resources to generate the highest level of support for its educational programmes. To do so, it has adopted an investment policy that is designed to give maximum return on its investment. This policy dictates investment in Repression Importers. In determining its investments, North Weeds is, however, quite neutral with respect to issues such as a company's labour practices. Indeed, this is quite proper. Not only should North Weeds invest its resources optimally, the demand that it be neutral precludes it from taking a stand on such issues. It may not take sides in such a dispute. The committee of concerned faculty responds simply that North Weeds has already taken sides. It is using its money in a way that benefits Repression Importers. That it has declined to change its policy also lends the university's prestige to the company. Neutrality is not an option for North Weeds. The only issue is which side to take.

The first thing to note about this dispute is that the university's claim to be neutral in the dispute and the concerned faculty's claim that it is not neutral are both correct. They are talking about different types of neutrality. North Weeds is claiming neutrality of position: they have not taken a position or adopted a policy about the labour practices of Repression Importers; they are merely acting on an investment policy that is quite neutral on such matters. The concerned faculty, however, is pointing out that whatever North Weeds' intentions are, its actions are having consequences for the issue. North Weeds is being accused of not being neutral $_c$. Both claims are true.

The next noteworthy feature of the dispute is that *under the circumstances* it is impossible, logically impossible, for North Weeds to be neutral $_c$. If North Weeds leaves its funds invested in Repression Importers, it enables them to continue their exploitive labour policies. If it withdraws its funds it will weaken Repression Importers and might cause them to reconsider their policies. Moreover, there is no alternative to simply continuing to invest with Repression Importers or acting to oppose their policies. There is no neutral $_c$ path of action available.

The final significant point is that impartial neutrality as I have expressed it does not preclude the university from taking positions on issues. It precludes the university from taking positions on issues in such a way as to determine or influence the views of members of the university community. It is quite possible, however, that North Weeds might decide that Repression Importers practises unjust labour policies and, thus, invest its funds elsewhere, without making any view concerning Repression Importers obligatory for its faculty or students. It can do this both because it does not require its faculty and students to comply or agree with its policy in order to implement it and because the issue concerns the institution's external affairs and thus has little potential impact on North Weeds' academic routine.

The real danger here is that rule (b), not rule (a), will be violated. North Weeds can, if it wishes, adopt a policy about investing in Repression Importers without making agreement with that policy obligatory for anyone except those who must execute it. It is not quite so easy to adopt such a policy without having a chilling effect on any potential debate on labour policies in the academic community of North Weeds. Faculty who may wish to express opinions or do research on the topic will now know that their employer has a view on the matter. The more timid among them may fear to challenge their employer's view. The more loyal among them may feel obliged to support it. The establishment of a policy can generate a climate of support for that policy, even if it is not made obligatory. Since the case under consideration is fictitious, and I am free to stipulate the facts, I will assume that this is not a problem.

What conclusions can be drawn from these facts? First, under the circumstances, North Weeds has a duty to take a stand. North Weeds is already entangled in the dispute. It cannot avoid affecting its outcome. Moreover, North Weeds can take a stand without substantially violating the kind of neutrality required of it – it can still be neutral ᵢ. Given that this is the case, a refusal to have a policy concerning investment in Repression Importers is equivalent to refusing to take responsibility for the consequences of one's acts.

We can also use these cases to discover some additional properties of university neutrality. We can express the principle involved in the above argument as an additional rule for impartial neutrality.

(e) *A university may take a stand on an issue in which it is entangled if it can do so without substantially violating rules (a) or (b).*

One additional rule is warranted. The world is full of significant issues and wrongs to be righted concerning which a university might be asked to have a position. If a university is to maintain the freedom of its intellectual climate, it must be clear that it cannot be expected to advocate every cause merely because that cause is righteous and just. It must be limited to taking a stand on issues in which it is already entangled. Thus:

(f) *A university may not take a stand on an issue gratuitously.*

The most serious objection to impartial neutrality as it has thus far been developed is that it is sterile. It tends to limit the university to the pursuit of academic questions and precludes it from doing good in the world except as that good is an accidental product of academic teaching and research. It may permit its members to devote their efforts to some cause, but it prohibits any decision by the institution to use its resources to accomplish some particular good. In short, it prohibits the service function of the university.

We have now returned to the problem posed by Professor DeGruve's case, and we are in a position to understand its structure more fully. When a university makes a decision to take on some particular social service, it must make a collective, rather than an individual, decision that this service is worth performing and worth performing in a particular way. The university cannot elect to train teachers without committing itself to the desirability of training teachers and of doing so in a certain way. Indeed, it must accept on the whole the desirability of the educational system for which these teachers are being trained.

A university cannot take on such a commitment without violating rule (b). Moreover, it is unlikely to escape violating rule (a) as well. Professor DeGruve has been put in a position where his views on teacher training have become a distinct liability to his participation in the accepted mission of his institution. Clearly, rule (b) has been violated. Innovation City has tried to defend itself from the charge of violating Professor DeGruve's academic freedom by holding that it has not, in fact, required him to accept any particular view. In effect, they have claimed that they have not violated rule (a). The viability of this claim depends on the dubious assumption that expecting one to act consistently on some view does not amount to a requirement to accept that view.

Mission-oriented enterprises thus inevitably violate impartial neutrality. The only questions are whether these violations are justified and whether they can be minimized. Consider first that the violation of impartial neutrality is neither incidental nor trivial. A university can, perhaps, have a view on a private corporation's labour practices without having an impact on the views of its members. It cannot, however, accept a mission without having an impact on the views of its members.

Moreover, the university cannot maintain exclusive control over the missions it accepts. It will not respond to every need. It will, instead, tend to respond to those needs that are identified as needs by those who are in a  position to articulate their needs, bring them to the university's attention and, above all, fund them. This means that the university will respond to public and private power. In short, a commitment to public service is not only a violation of the kind of neutrality required by academic freedom, but is potentially a serious violation. It can make a university highly subservient to current interests.

I shall argue that despite these contentions, *mission-oriented enterprises are legitimate activities for universities, provided they are reasonable extensions of the university's primary functions of research and teaching, that they are selected in a legitimate way, and that the conflict with academic freedom is minimal.* I shall return to these qualifications shortly. We need first to state the positive argument.

The basic argument for this view is simply that there is much good to be done in the world that universities can do and do best, and that this good will not be done unless universities deliberately set out to do it. This claim, unhappily, requires an extensive defence, which I cannot give here. I shall confine myself to one line of argument. It is important to remember the extent to which democratic and technological societies depend on knowledge. In this context it is important to remember this because it suggests that the question is not whether the knowledge-dependent services that universities provide are to be provided – they are necessary and will be provided somewhere by someone. The real question is whether knowledge-based services will be provided by universities or by other kinds of institutions. In a world where universities did not provide teaching and research directed to particular social and economic needs, such teaching and research would occur elsewhere.

This being the case, there are excellent reasons for locating such enterprises in universities. Universities provide a healthy and liberalizing context for such teaching and research. They make it possible to look at what is done from a variety of perspectives, and they make it difficult to approach a problem with only a narrow set of interests. By contrast, we may be sure that if training and research are to be done by private corporations, they will rarely be judged by criteria beyond the economic interests of the corporations that provide them. When a corporation does research aimed toward, let us say, developing a device to pick apples, it is likely to ask questions focused on problems of engineering and marketing. It is unlikely to exhibit great concern for the effects of the device on agricultural labour or the ecology. The same project done in a decent university is far more likely to have to confront this broader range of issues.

Further, knowledge produced in a university is more likely to be broadly and democratically available than if it is produced elsewhere. The same considerations that argue against suppressing ideas also argue against withholding them. Knowledge produced at a university is not normally held to be the private possession of its producer. It will normally be publicly available both to the researcher's professional peers and to the general public.

Finally, we should not lose sight of the extent to which support for the university in our society is contingent on the perception that it produces and disseminates useful knowledge. We must ask ourselves what kind of support will be available if universities are perceived as places where only academic questions are asked and applicable knowledge occurs only as an unintended by-product. I suspect that under such conditions support will be meagre.

In short, a university's decision to meet an identified social or economic need may exact a cost on the purity with which academic freedom can be maintained. It also has the consequence of broadening the range of concerns to which the ideals of academic freedom can be applied. Knowledge production in the society at large will be more open when it is accomplished in universities, even if universities lose some of their openness as a consequence. The alternative may be a free, but small university system located in a society whose practical knowledge is generated by comparatively closed and narrowly focused institutions.

I also believe that there are some epistemological virtues that arise from the inclusion of mission-oriented activities within the university. The basic assumption of this chapter is that the primary question to be asked when trying to decide how a university should conduct its affairs concerns the conditions that promote inquiry. A commitment to mission-oriented enterprises has appeared a liability in this regard since it has the potential to weaken the university's neutrality. But such a commitment may also be an asset because it can keep academic questions from becoming dissociated from real human problems and important human questions. One of the dangers faced by academic disciplines, particularly in the humanities and social sciences, when they are enclosed in an academic setting, is the tendency to lose contact with the human setting that gave rise to them. One of the things that impresses me (in retrospect) about the philosophical tradition in which I was trained is the degree to which the concern for analysing language had lost contact with human problems. There is, for example, a vast literature in American philosophy of education on the concept of teaching that is notable both for its sophistication and for its lack of potential to illuminate the activity of teaching. There is another body of literature in epistemology that has only the most tenuous connection with science or mathematics. Theoretical inquiry need not be palatable to 'practical people'. When it is successful it will provide new and more profound ways of seeing the world, ways that may be troubling or offensive. That is what thought should do and that is why 'practical people' must not have great power over it. But when theoretical inquiry generates concepts that no longer seem to provide ways of seeing the world at all, it has become corrupt. Isolation of theoretical inquiry from human affairs has the potential to produce just this sort of intellectual decadence.

If neutrality is understood in a way that precludes involvement by the university in human affairs, it will tend to turn theoretical inquiry into a kind of intellectual game. Inquiry will not be aided if irrelevance is the price of independence. These arguments indicate that the trick to maintaining a healthy climate for fruitful theoretical inquiry is to find ways that promote the involvement of scholars in human affairs and also maintain the independence of inquiry.

I have suggested that mission-oriented enterprises are legitimate activities for universities subject to three conditions: that they be extensions of the university's primary functions of research and teaching, that they be selected in a legitimate way, and that they generate minimal conflict with academic freedom. These conditions are the key to involvement with independence.

Any mission accepted by a university must be subservient to the set of values that govern its primary functions of inquiry and teaching. A university is not a mere purveyor of techniques. It has no business in providing training programmes unless inquiry is a part of that training. When it becomes a purveyor of techniques, it risks sacrificing its independence without any corresponding benefits. Universities may appropriately train lawyers or teachers because theoretical inquiry about law or education is a reasonable part of such training. Universities should not train professional athletes. One of the major scandals of American universities is the kind of commitment they have made to intercollegiate sports. Having built immense stadiums and committed vast funds to sports programmes, they find themselves under immense pressure to win. Such pressure is rarely affected by such trivialities as academic goals. Thus, universities with large athletic budgets routinely admit academically unqualified athletes, develop courses for them to pass to maintain their eligibility, and pressure faculty to reduce demands on them. I know of one case (happily, elsewhere than Cornell) in which a faculty member was literally fired by the football coach for 'upsetting' a player with a radical idea. Such abuses are loudly bemoaned. That they have their roots in universities taking on a public service (entertainment) that is foreign to their central function, is not.

That mission-oriented enterprises must be consistent with the university's central functions also means that universities cannot be expected to provide research or teaching to pre-specified goals without subjecting these goals to criticism. The commitment to inquiry requires that the university be capable of reflecting on ends as well as means. A society may ask a university to train teachers, but in doing so it must also recognize that a university is a place that must reflect on its endeavours. If teachers are to be trained, teaching and education must be thought about. Society's view of the sort of teacher it wants may be criticized or rejected. Free inquiry demands that a university's missions be assessed, not just accomplished. A university is not merely a supplier of knowledge and teaching for ends supplied it.

The demand that service enterprises be consistent with the ideal of inquiry also precludes the university from accepting enterprises that cannot be freely or openly debated or discussed. Universities ought not to do military research if the results of that research will be classified. Generally, whatever work a university does, the ideas produced must be freely available for criticism.

Making sure that those services that it targets to particular social needs are a rational extension of its central goals and ideals is the central point in having universities that serve society without losing their intellectual independence. When both universities and their clients understand that a university will only engage in some service activity when free and open inquiry is seen as contributing to that activity, the university is less likely than otherwise to find its freedom eroded by the missions it has accepted.

The second condition of accepting a mission is that it be legitimately chosen. Recall that one objection to universities taking on service activities is that these activities tend to lead the university to attend to the needs of those who have the power to express their needs. The university may thus come to have its agenda of concerns defined by society's rich and powerful. It is inappropriate to respond to this problem by demanding that universities must avoid subservience to power or wealth by making an independent assessment of what needs are legitimately met. To decide to devote the institution's resources to support 'progressive' causes requires an official view of what causes are progressive and is a violation of impartial neutrality.

There are, however, two plausible responses to the problem. First, it is important that members of a university community have the freedom to devote themselves to serving some needs with which they personally identify. It is also important that universities have sources of funding for projects that they control and are not dependent on funding sources external to the university. The university's capacity to respond to the needs of people who are not financially or politically able to create a demand that their needs be attended to will substantially depend on the availability of funds for faculty willing to devote their attention to such needs.

The second response to the problem is to insist that the

process whereby society identifies tasks for the university to perform be legitimate. By legitimate I mean suitably democratic. When a university decides to engage in some form of social service, it also elects to share some power over its enterprises with agencies external to the university. This external power will characteristically be political power. Thus, a university is likely to be able to respond to the needs of people other than society's rich and powerful to the extent that the society's political process is sensitive to their needs. Universities have a right to expect that those services asked of it be determined in a satisfactory democratic fashion and a duty to resist when they are not.

It is worth adding that the legitimacy of a university's social services must inevitably depend to a great degree on the legitimacy of authority in the society in which the university exists. I find the kinds of relations that obtain between universities and governments in Western democracies generally acceptable because I believe these governments to be legitimate and suitably democratic. To one who regards such governments as oppressive and undemocratic, the efforts of universities to serve needs identified by these governments will seem equally oppressive and undemocratic. In a repressive society, the intellectual vitality of a university is perhaps best measured by the degree to which its members are in conflict with the authorities.

To summarize: the second condition that a university's social services should meet is that the means whereby they are identified and funded should be democratic and should admit of diversity.

The third condition is that conflicts with academic freedom should be minimal. Recall the source of the problem. It is difficult for a university to accept some mission without also accepting the legitimacy of that mission and a view of how the mission is to be performed. Moreover, these commitments are likely to be translated into commitments that are obligatory for the faculty responsible for performing the mission. What are we to say here?

The basic claim I shall defend is that the right of the individual faculty member to academic freedom is legitimately balanced against the need for a university to pursue a given mission, provided that such conflicts can be minimized and that the diversity of the institution as a whole is not thereby reduced. The components of the argument for this claim have already been developed. The first is that social service activities are an important component of a university's life. They enhance not only its utility, but its intellectual life as well. This establishes their value. The second point is that academic freedom is justified by utilitarian arguments. It is a right established to accomplish a given end. However, it is not a right that is the right of every moral agent. Philosophically, this is of utmost importance in deciding whether it is proper to balance a right against the desire to accomplish some good. Those rights that people have because they are moral agents are fundamental rights of every person. It is normally improper to trade them off for other kinds of benefits, particularly when those benefits do not accrue to the person who is losing the right. Slavery violates a fundamental right, the right to self-ownership. It would not be justified if it could be shown to be economically desirable. It would not be justified even if those made slaves were better off economically.

Academic freedom, however, is not absolute. It is a right extended to a particular group of people for a particular purpose. It is a right of university faculty because it promotes the growth of knowledge. Because the right is justified by the ends it serves and because it is not a fundamental right to which everyone is entitled, it may be modified or withheld when it fails to serve its intended ends or when those ends themselves are superseded by others. It is, thus, reasonably reconsidered when there is something legitimate to be accomplished thereby. Given that a university's missions are something legitimate to be accomplished, the right of academic freedom may be reassessed in that light. Academic freedom is nonetheless vitally important to universities, so conflicts with it must be minimal and its basic purpose still served.

I have two strategies for reconciling the university's social services with academic freedom. Concerning individual faculty members, I believe the basic strategy for minimizing conflict between academic freedom and social services is to insist that when there is a need to have people who accept the goals and approaches of an enterprise, such acceptance should be pursued by hiring and by incentives, rather than by termination or coercion. When a university needs a contingent of suitably devoted folk to accomplish something in particular, it may hire them or offer inducements to its current staff. Other things being equal, this should suffice to assure people properly devoted to the university's missions. On the other hand, universities should not be permitted to terminate or coerce their current faculty to gain acceptance of some mission. This will provide adequate opportunity for individuals to refuse or abandon a task when they are not persuaded of its merits.

The second strategy is to insist that a university's missions be linked with non-mission-oriented academic programmes whose members are not expected to be subservient to any mission. Universities should be expected to institutionalize pockets of potential diversity and criticism within any mission-oriented enterprise. Teachers, for example, should be trained where education is studied. This suggests that a faculty of education ought to consist of two types of people. On one hand, there must be some people whose primary responsibility is to provide prospective teachers with those skills they will employ in the classroom. These people must work together, must share some common views concerning how teachers are to be trained, and must accommodate themselves to the current legislative standards for the certification of teachers. Some commitment to a collective view of how teachers are to be trained is a reasonable expectation. On the other hand, there ought also to be people whose basic responsibility is the theoretical study of education. Here no collective agreement on how teachers are to be trained is required. When these two types of individuals are both engaged in the training and education of teachers, the prospects of the institution's mission being served in a way that conflicts minimally with academic freedom are good. Maintaining such a mix of personnel allows a university to institutionalize both a commitment to its mission and the capacity to be critical of it.

These strategies are intended to be illustrative of the ways in which the values of academic freedom can be balanced against and reconciled with the desire to perform some mission. They are obviously neither exhaustive nor particularly detailed. They do, however, exemplify some basic principles. Universities are fundamentally institutions that exist to promote the growth of knowledge. The pursuit of truth is their central commitment. When the university seeks to achieve worthy goals that go beyond this central commitment, it may and should do so when these goals are a reasonable extension of its central purpose and when they do not undermine the climate of freedom and diversity. Freedom and diversity are properties that are required for the university as a whole. They are, however, instrumental values and are not fundamental rights of individuals. It is thus permissible for a university to have variations in the nature and degree of academic freedom available to its members *if* it can do so without sacrificing the general climate of freedom and diversity in the institution. The strategies I have suggested indicate that this is possible.

Consider now the second hard case. Professor Sater has been let go by his institution because he is regarded as an incompetent philosopher. The curious thing is that Professor Sater is regarded as perfectly competent by those who do the same kind of philosophy that he does. He has the misfortune to be evaluated, however, by those from another philosophical club. We must also give Professor Sater's colleagues the benefit of a doubt. I assume that they are not out to get Professor Sater because he is an existentialist. They appear to have shown a desire to have a competent existentialist on their faculty. Rather, they genuinely believe that Professor Sater is not a competent philosopher. The circumstances thus appear to be that Professor Sater's philosophical ability is seen quite differently by different philosophers in a way that depends on their own training and philosophical perspectives.

How is this a problem for academic freedom? Recall that I expressed a central principle of academic freedom as follows: scholars may not be rewarded, denied rewards or punished on account of the views they express, but may be rewarded, or denied awards or punished on account of the competence with which they argue their views. Professor Sater can appeal to this principle to argue that his right to academic freedom has been violated. His argument would maintain that his competence is not in question. His record of research and publications and the approval of his work by other existentialist philosophers demonstrates that he is a competent existentialist. He is not being let go because he is incompetent. He is being let go because he is an existentialist. Thus, he is being punished on account of his opinions, not his competence. This is a clear violation of academic freedom.

Professor Sater's colleagues in philosophy at Stationary University will, however, not see themselves as rejecting existentialism *per se*. Rather, they will argue that philosophy has certain standards for what counts as a good argument and what counts as an acceptable use of language. Professor Sater often seems not to construct arguments at all. He seems rather concerned to describe some facet of existence by means of a vocabulary created especially for that purpose. This appears to his colleagues to be needlessly obscure and to fall far short of the standards of clarity extant in Anglo-American philosophy. They will, therefore, hold that they are responding to Professor Sater's competence. That he is an existentialist does not figure in their deliberations.

Who is right? I believe that there is no answer to this question – for epistemological reasons that render problematic the general principle that universities may reward or punish competence but not opinion. The difficulty is that the principle assumes that a person's competence can be judged independently of his beliefs. That is often true, but often it is not true. Sometimes a person's substantive commitments are so intertwined with procedure in his field that it becomes impossible to distinguish judgements of competence from disagreement on substance. Let us see why. Consider the following two arguments:

A.   All felines hate water.
     Tigers are felines.
     Therefore, tigers hate water.
B.   All cats have fur.
     Figaro has fur.
     Therefore, Figaro is a cat.

These arguments differ in two ways. Argument A is valid (the conclusion follows from the premises), but its conclusion is false. Some tigers appear to love water. Argument B is invalid (the conclusion does not follow from the premises), but its conclusion is true. (Figaro is my cat.) The distinction between the validity of arguments and the truth of the conclusions of an argument provides a way to sharpen the distinction between judgements of competence and disagreements with a person's views. We might hold that any field will have a set of standards that will define the validity of arguments in a field. Such standards will simultaneously define what counts as competence. A competent person is one who can construct valid arguments. Disagreements concerning opinions or viewpoints, however, are disagreements concerning the conclusions of arguments.

No doubt this account is too simple and to make it fully adequate would require a lengthy discussion. I do, however, believe that this distinction, or one much like it, is at the heart of the view that one can reasonably differentiate between judgements of competence and differences of view. If this is correct, it then becomes possible to show its major difficulty and to show where it cannot coherently be applied. Its major difficulty is that it assumes a sharp distinction between the methodology of a field and the substantive viewpoint of a field. I have already argued at length that this is a dubious distinction. Some of the substantive commitments of a field are part of its methodology. Such commitments set a field's problems and define the criteria for their solution. One cannot, therefore, assume that a field's logic is one thing and its conclusions another.

It does not follow from this that the distinction between a person's competence and the views he holds is without merit. In many fields there is reasonable agreement concerning which assumptions form part of the field's methodology and which are open issues and plausible objects of inquiry. When there is such agreement – when, in Kuhn's terms, a field has a common paradigm – there is no great problem in distinguishing between disagreements and judgements of competence. I do not mean by this that reasonable people will not sometimes disagree about someone's competence or that judgements as to who is competent or who is not can be made with exactness. The application of sophisticated and complex standards must inevitably be difficult and inexact. The element of judgement cannot be removed from this application. What I do mean is that the distinction between judgements of competence and disagreements concerning particular views have a coherent meaning, so long as and to the extent that a field has a coherent and adequately accepted consensus on what assumptions are presupposed in its work and what questions are open to investigation.

But this is precisely what many fields lack. Some fields, like physics, have achieved a degree of consensus on fundamental principles. Physicists may disagree, and they may be organized into sub-groups. But their sub-groups are not usually a function of their disagreements. Rather, such groupings reflect differing interests and a division of labour. Even when physicists do take sides on some issue, they retain enough in common to be able to judge arguments for each side. Serious confusion about the standards of the field are likely to occur only occasionally when some very central claim of the field has come under attack. Fields such as psychology or philosophy, however, are characterized by enduring fundamental disagreements about the nature of the field and about acceptable standards for it. They have multiple paradigms, with no common view of the field. Its practitioners will systematically disagree on what counts as the open problems of the field and on how these problems are to be solved. Moreover, to the degree that there are multiple paradigms the adherents of one will tend to see the adherents of the others as incompetent. They will see them as lacking a grasp on what the field's problems are or on how they should be approached.

This is presumably the problem that Professor Sater has encountered. The sense of method embedded in the view of the field shared by Anglo-American analytic philosophers assumes that many philosophical problems are problems having to do with the meaning of words. The set of commitments generating this interest in language also make clarity and precision of language major methodological considerations. It is widely held that many philosophical muddles result from inadequate attention to how words are used. Professor Sater, however, has been trained in a view that is most concerned to provide rich and provocative descriptions of the lived world. The assessment of the language employed is not so much in terms of its clarity and precision as in terms of its ability to focus attention on hard-to-see features of our experience. In order to do this, language is often used in a highly metaphorical or unusual way.

In short, the standards of these two sorts of philosophy are not only different, they conflict in ways rooted in substantive differences about the nature and tasks of the field. An individual who has learned one perspective is strongly predisposed to find the procedures of the other bizzarre and absurd. From the perspective of an analytic philosopher, finding a competent existentialist is only a little easier than finding a round square.

Under these circumstances *there is a deep epistemological problem in applying the principle of academic freedom, for its application depends on our ability to distinguish between disagreements and judgements of competence. But where there is no agreement on the paradigm, there cannot be agreement on how this distinction is to be applied.* The case of Professor Sater is, I believe, the hardest hard case. It is, in fact, not decidable, since the very standards for judging competence are in doubt.

It is important at this point to disavow two potential solutions to this dilemma. The first solution is to suggest that the decision concerning Professor Sater depends essentially on whose view of the field is correct. If the view of Professor Sater's colleagues is correct, Professor Sater is incompetent. If existentialism is correct, Professor Sater's academic freedom has been violated. This solution has the liability of being impossible because, at the moment, the question of who is right cannot be decided. I do not mean by this that the intellectual issues that divide divergent approaches within a field cannot be rationally adjudicated. They can. Rather, the point is that this has not been accomplished. As long as the field is, in fact, divided on its fundamental principles, it is not possible to achieve a defensible judgement on a person's competence where what is at stake is the selection of fundamental principles. People must be evaluated on standards that exist, not on ones that might exist.

The second kind of solution is one of tolerance. One might hold that when a field is genuinely divided on fundamental principles the solution is to evaluate individuals in terms of the principles they accept. Existentialists should be evaluated on the criteria appropriate to existentialism by existentialists. Analytic philosophers should be evaluated on criteria appropriate to analytic philosophy by analytic philosophers. Presumably, in judging a person's competence the duty is to evaluate people on appropriate standards and have people who understand these standards do the evaluation. Professor Sater was hired because he was an existentialist. In hiring him, his colleagues also implicitly recognized existentialism as a legitimate form of philosophy. Recognizing it as legitimate is not the same as agreeing with it. Rather, it is a matter of noting that it continues to have respect in the field and continues to retain sufficient intellectual cohesion such that a reasonable person might be persuaded by it. If Professor Sater's colleagues did not regard existentialism as having legitimacy of this sort, they should not have hired him. In not promoting him once he had demonstrated that he was a competent existentialist, Professor Sater's colleagues changed the rules. They restricted the commitment to the legitimacy of existentialism that was implicit in their hiring him. Having once recognized the legitimacy of existentialism, Professor Sater's colleagues had a duty to evaluate him on criteria appropriate to existentialism.

This argument is a successful defence of Professor Sater, but it depends on the appeal to the notion of due process – it is a violation of Professor Sater's right to fairness to change the rules in the middle of the game. I also believe that tolerance is in order when there are competing standards in a field and where each set of standards can make a case for legitimacy. I believe this is the case for Professor Sater. Existentialism is a legitimate form of philosophy. Insofar as this is true, its practitioners should be evaluated on its criteria.

A general policy of tolerance is, however, not defensible, for it fails to recognize that not all diversity of standards is diversity between legitimate options, and it makes change in the standards of a field unduly difficult. Consider how the standards of a field might change. It will be convenient here to put it schematically. Suppose that at some time, $t_1$, the standards of a field are $A$, but at $t_2$ they have become $B$. How might the transition from $A$ to $B$ occur?

One response is that all of the members of the field who held $A$ at $t_1$ were persuaded of $B$ by $t_2$. The change of standards of the field is, thus, a function of the change of the views of its members. It is most important here to understand that this is rarely a sufficient account of such a change. Intellectual changes must involve change of mind. Some member of the field must conceive and promote $B$ and must win some support among the members of the field for it. Once $B$ has achieved a 'critical mass' of adherents, however, other mechanisms of change become possible. $B$'s adherents may begin to inhabit positions of power and influence in their field. They may become the editors of journals. They may come to occupy the senior positions at universities and thus determine who is hired, who is promoted and how novices in the field are trained, and they may become the givers of grants and the awarders of academic honours. When this has occurred, power in the field has changed hands. There is little need to persuade those who continue to adhere to $A$. They no longer referee the intellectual life of the field, and they will increasingly find themselves excluded from it. They will grow old, become inactive, retire, and die. The field belongs to the adherents of $B$, who will have captured it not necessarily by being more persuasive than the adherents of $A$, but by being younger.

One additional set of concepts is necessary if we are to get a firm grasp of the problem of tolerance and academic freedom. Whenever a field changes its collective opinion about any idea, including its fundamental principles, a new idea must first be proposed. It must get on the field's agenda. Having reached the field's agenda, it must then be selected. We should, therefore, distinguish two phases in the emergence of a new idea: its proposal and its selection.

What role does tolerance play in an intellectual change that involves a fundamental change in the basic commitments of a field? This question can profitably be put as a question about different levels of tolerance. Suppose, then, we ask about the consequences of high tolerance versus low tolerance on the process of intellectual change.

The consequences of a very low level of tolerance should be obvious enough. New ideas will have a hard time getting on the agenda of a field and once on will have a hard time getting accepted. Allowed to persist, a condition of excessively low tolerance will cause a field to degenerate into obscurity and irrelevance. It will begin to accumulate problems that it cannot solve on its current assumptions. Its attempts to solve such problems will be increasingly forced, *ad hoc*, vague or obscure.

It must be insisted, however, that excessive tolerance can also retard intellectual progress. The difficulty with high tolerance is that while it is easy to get new ideas, even profoundly radical ones, on a field's agenda, it is nearly impossible to get them off.

*Excessive tolerance makes the process of intellectual selection
difficult.* It can  promote a situation of intellectual anarchy
where it becomes difficult to apply any standards, reasonable or
otherwise, and where no idea, no matter how unworthy, ever
suffers the pain of intellectual rejection. In such cases fields
change and ideas may be subject to fads or external pressures.
But they do not progress.

This point can be argued from another angle. Consider the
matter from the perspective of the kinds of arguments that can
be made that one's views should be tolerated. I have argued that
Professor Sater should be tolerated because he is a competent
practitioner of a legitimate philosophical style. The difficulty
with this sort of argument is that it is easily appropriated by
those to whom it would be intellectually disastrous to apply it.
Consider how the argument might be applied by an astrologer
seeking employment in an astronomy department. 'I am a
competent astrologer,' he might claim. 'I am so regarded by my
fellow astrologers. I have published extensively in my field and
am well regarded by my peer group. That astronomy depart-
ments will not hire me or other astrologers is not a function of
our competence. It is a function of the fact that astrologers
employ a different paradigm from astronomers. Intellectual
tolerance, however, demands that we be evaluated on criteria
appropriate to astrologers by astrologers.'

I assume that his argument is spurious. Astrology is a
thoroughly disreputable enterprise, there is no such thing as a
competent astrologer, and the very fact that a person is an
astrologer disqualifies him from being appointed (as an
astrologer) to a position in an educational institution. This
illustration thus indicates that tolerance cannot be a universal
policy whenever we have a case where individuals claim to be
working in a different paradigm. *A general policy of tolerance is
too pervasive. It prevents the rejection of a point of view by a field,
no matter how disreputable that point of view has become.*

What follows? Put simply, in the sort of hard case where not
only a person's competence but also the standards according to
which he is to be judged are at issue, there are two extremes to be
avoided. One may not assume that where there are multiple
paradigms the correct one must be chosen and used to judge a
person's work. That option will arbitrarily close open issues and

truncate fruitful debate. Legitimate diversity needs to be tolerated. At the same time, one may not assume that 'all paradigms are created equal' and that people must always judge people by their own standards. That option will arbitrarily keep open issues that should be closed and allow profitable debate to degenerate into an intellectual Babel. The alternative, of course, is to decide. When someone like Professor Sater appeals for tolerance, there is a decision to be made by those who must judge Professor Sater and who do not share his view of their field as to whether his view is worthy of tolerance. Such choices can be made.

It should be noted that implicit in the discussion of multiple paradigms are two distinguishable cases. Professor Sater's case involves a situation that might be called a case of coexisting paradigms. Anglo-American philosophy has often been different from Continental philosophy. Here are two traditions with their own histories. At some periods they interact fruitfully, at others they appear almost as separate disciplines. Such coexisting paradigms seem common in the behavioural sciences and the humanities. The other case is one of intellectual transition. When one paradigm is being replaced by another, there will be a point at which the field has multiple paradigms. In such cases, however, this is unlikely to be an enduring feature of the field.

When there are coexisting paradigms, the question to be asked is whether a given approach is in fact a viable approach to some reasonable subject matter. Given that there are multiple paradigms this question will be difficult, but not impossible, to answer. Intellectual standards may vary according to one's perspective, but intellectual standards are not packaged into self-contained, mutually exclusive, intellectual boxes. Different enterprises will have points in common. There will be some intellectual standards that are widely applicable. Often some points of view can be identified as disreputable. Astrology, for example, lacks procedures to settle disputes among its own practitioners. Moreover, it rests on a view of the cosmos that is known to be false as surely as anything is known to be false. Existentialism, by contrast, exhibits no such signs of disreputability. It has a recognizable point and recognizable strategies for pursuing its objectives. It makes assumptions that

are questionable. I suspect they are wrong. That is why I am not
an existentialist. But they are not known to be false, and one can
see that a competent person might accept them.

Similar points can be made concerning cases of intellectual
transition. When a paradigm has lost its grip on a field and has
acquired competition, intellectual standards in the field will
become problematic. It does not follow that everything is in
doubt and that it is impossible to give reasons for preferring one
view to another. Again, the point is that judgements concerning
the worth of alternative or competing approaches can be made.
*It is wrong to make them prematurely in a way that closes
potentially fruitful debate and interaction, but it is also a mistake
to refuse to make judgements when they are warranted. The first is
the path to intellectual atrophy. The second is the path to
intellectual anarchy. Neither is compatible with the growth of
knowledge.*

I know of no way to turn these claims into procedures or
criteria so that it will be clear to everyone exactly when tolerance
of different approaches is in order and when it is not. There is a
lengthy epistemological discussion possible that might give the
reader a better grasp of what is involved, but that is beyond the
purposes of this enterpise and, thus, I shall forbear. It is
important to note, however, that the fact that in the cases under
consideration intellectual standards themselves are at issue
makes such decisions difficult and mistakes likely.

This seems to me to underscore the importance of peer
judgement in academic evaluation. This may, at first, seem
mistaken . After all, it is through the process of peer judgement
that the adherents of one perspective can   exercise their
authority over adherents of another. Is this not what the case of
Professor Sater suggests? The danger is clearly real. There are,
however, two considerations in favour of peer judgement, even
in such cases. The weaker of the two is simply that academics are
not any less capable of tolerance when appropriate than anyone
else. One should not simply assume that they will take every
opportunity to enforce their own views when tolerance is in
order. The basic consideration, however, is that there is really no
one else to give the responsibility to. In such cases a scholar's
peers may be inappropriately intolerant of his work, but who
else is there to make a judgement? How will deans or

administrators make it? In an institution whose commitment is the pursuit of truth, peer judgement, flawed as it may be, is the only way to bring expertise to bear on the evaluation of professional competence. A scholar's peers at least have the virtue of having achieved an understanding of a field and the debates and alternatives within it.

*Peer judgement is, thus, the citadel of academic authority and academic freedom. It is essential to the growth of knowledge because it is the way in which ideas are judged on their merits.* It must also be recognized, however, that academic judgements are never terribly clear. In the cases I have been discussing they may be terribly unclear. It follows that an institution committed to peer judgement must have some tolerance for mistakes, or at least for judgements that can be made reasonable, but never highly persuasive. It does not, however, follow that such institutions must tolerate unfairness. A judgement that is conscientiously made but proves wrong is a mistake. It must be distinguished from cases where people are judged capriciously or on the basis of race or sex. These are injustices. Procedures for the protection of people against unfairness can and should be designed. They are, in fact, essential. Universities, after all, should be committed to justice, as well as truth. The trick is to design ways to evaluate people that promote fairness but that do not do so at the price of peer judgement and end up placing responsibility for the intellectual life of an institution in the hands of administrators.

I am aware of one institution in the United States that has designed a purely mechanical system for some of its judgements of faculty performance. Teachers give rating forms to their students. Their scholarly production is measured by a formula that assigns a number to a given article with due consideration to its length, character and the prestige of the journal where it appeared. Such numbers are integrated into a formula that generates a rating suitable for giving raises or promotions. In some parts of the world, faculty appointments and promotions are covered by detailed civil service rules. Such systems may be admirable in their ability to provide job security and to prevent arbitrary judgements. They can also exact a high price of peer judgement. It needs again to be affirmed that peer judgement is an indispensable part of the way in which ideas are assessed and knowledge grows. By all means, it should be as fair as possible. But it is essential to intellectual communities and cannot be allowed to become victim of a penchant for bureaucratic and rule-governed deliberations.

Consider one final case. I have suggested the case of Professor Dete was unproblematic. It is a clear case of a violation of academic freedom that raises few difficult philosophical questions. Professor Dete, although a competent economist, is being threatened because he holds an unpopular view. We may, however, make the case more interesting by altering the facts. Let us suppose that Professor Dete is denied promotion or tenure by his professional colleagues. When asked to justify their action, they claim that the fact that Professor Dete had written from a Marxist point of view formed no part of their judgement. Rather, they considered only the quality of the scholarship involved in the development of the arguments. They summarize their views in the following words: 'Our rejection of Professor Dete is based entirely on his qualities as a scholar. We have not considered his views, however offensive they may be to some of us. Rather, we find Professor Dete's work deficient in a number of important respects. His selection of problems and their conceptualization is poor. He has chosen not to pursue issues that appear to have promise to advance his field, and he conceptualizes the problems he does work on in ways that render him unable to employ some of the more sophisticated techniques of the field. Moreover, his arguments are full of remarks that are irrelevant to economic analysis. Professor Dete sometimes seems unable to decide whether he is an economist, a philosopher, an historian or a journalist. Whatever he is, he is not a competent economist.'

Professor Dete responds as follows: 'It may well be that according to the standards of capitalist economists, I am incompetent. That, however, says far more about the academic standards of bourgeois professors in capitalist countries than it says about the quality of my mind or my work. Progressive economists should not expect their work to be admired by those who are intellectual captives of the privileged classes and whose work supports the oppression of working people. My work is well regarded by progressive elements. That is enough for me.'

Let us assume that both Professor Dete and his colleagues are sincere in their judgement and accurate in their facts. How, then, shall we conceive the dispute? Certainly it is not the simple violation of academic freedom that the previous variant of Professor Dete's case was. Professor Dete's colleagues are judging the competence of his work, not his conclusions. This variant of the Dete case appears to have most in common with the case of Professor Sater. It is a conflict that arises from the existence of different paradigms within a field. Professor Dete is a Marxist. He does not share the neo-classical paradigm of many Western economists and of his colleagues. His colleagues, judging his work by their standards, regard him as incompetent.

It is, however, important to distinguish this variant of Professor Dete's case from Professor Sater's case. In the conflict between analytic philosophers and existentialists, reasons could be given for regarding both traditions as intellectually respectable. While analytic philosophers may not share the intellectual commitments or aspirations of existentialists, neither are they in a position to treat them as disreputable. Adherents of these different traditions thus have an obligation to tolerate one another. Professor Dete, however, has given reasons to believe that his colleagues' point of view is disreputable. Moreover, his argument, if it can be generalized to any degree, is most destructive to the analysis of academic freedom I have developed.

Professor Dete's arguments can be resolved into two basic claims. The first is that the very questions and methods of the dominant paradigm in economics support the interests of capitalists against those of the working class. Note that Dete's claim is far stronger than the claim that contemporary economists happen to hold some conclusions that he considers inimical to the interests of workers. He claims that oppression inheres not only in *what* economists think but in *how* they think.

Professor Dete's second claim is that the intellectual standards of the dominant school of economics do not change in response to appropriate factors. Rather, the standards of the discipline are subservient to the interests of the dominant classes. This claim assumes a distinction that needs some discussion. It is also, unfortunately, a distinction that presupposes some epistemological views that are difficult and controversial and that cannot be adequately treated here. I have assumed throughout this volume that a field's questions, methods and standards evolve. I have generally talked as though this evolution were a rational process. But, of course, this is not necessarily so. A field's standards may change, or not change, in response to influences or pressures that are less than rational.

I cannot do justice to the distinction between rational and non-rational influences here. I can only illustrate it. Sometimes a field's basic assumptions prove unfruitful. They may generate more problems than they solve, or they may prove inconsistent with something else people have discovered. Change in a field in response to such factors is rational change. On the other hand, the basic assumptions of a field may change or not change because they have become entangled in external political or economic interests. The belief that acquired characteristics can be inherited survived in the Soviet Union long after it had been abandoned in the West because Stalin believed the view to be important to Marxism and enforced it on Soviet science. Such influences typify non-rational considerations.

Professor Dete has maintained that the standards and basic assumptions of contemporary economics are captive to such a set of non-rational considerations. They are what they are because they serve the interests of the dominant classes. It is to be noted that Professor Dete's claim is merely an instance of a quite general one commonly made by Marxists. There are, according to some Marxist theoreticians, not only capitalist economics, but capitalist art, capitalist philosophy and capitalist physics. The entire realm of intellectual discourse, it seems, is politically infested and made to order for the interests of capitalists.

This line of argument, if correct, is absolutely fatal to the view of academic freedom I have developed, which sees universities as places where truth is pursued. It requires that scholars be free from external pressure in order to follow the evidence and the argument where they lead. And it regards the enforcement of current academic standards as not only legitimate but part of the mechanism for promoting the growth of knowledge.

But Professor Dete has pointed to an argument that suggests that this view of current universities is fundamentally wrong. It is not just that individuals in the university occasionally or even frequently are induced or intimidated into serving prevailing political or economic interests. Such occurrences are violations of academic freedom, but they are not problems with its conception. Rather, the very standards of rationality to which universities struggle to adhere turn out to serve not truth, but class interests. Indeed, the very notion of academic freedom, because it permits and legitimates the enforcement of these corrupt intellectual standards, turns out to be nothing more than a subterfuge cloaking bourgeois interests with the language of liberty.

This argument cannot be answered in the brief space I have to give it. It would require a separate treatise. I have raised it because it is an important problem and because it illuminates a basic assumption of academic freedom. *Academic freedom assumes the legitimacy and rationality of the intellectual standards universities employ. These standards are, however, changeable human artifacts. It is not an absurd or incoherent idea that they can become subservient to external interests.* Indeed, there are numerous historical cases where just this sort of thing has happened. (Marxist societies provide many of the better current examples.) Intellectual standards can be corrupt. When they are, academic freedom will do little to promote the pursuit of truth.

On the other hand, I find the general form of the Marxist argument most implausible. It is not silly to suggest that there is such a thing as bourgeois philosophy. It is (currently) silly to suggest that there are bourgeois physics or chemistry. The independence of the world views of the physical and biological sciences from political bias is adequately testified to by the fact that they are the same the world over. These considerations do, at least, show that it cannot simply be presumed that the intellectual standards of any discipline are corrupt because that discipline is practised in a capitalist country. Arguments that the intellectual standards of a field are captive to political or class interests need to be made in detail on a case-by-case basis.

Finally, I find the kind of argument given by Professor Dete to be dubious because it does not ring true in my own field of philosophy. One can trace the origins of much of contemporary Anglo-American philosophy to the empiricism of the last several centuries, and it is true that the view of knowledge of empiricist philosophers such as Locke and Mill influenced their political philosophies and supported the growth of liberal and capitalist ideologies. But it is also true that there were profound intellectual grounds for these doctrines in developments of the natural sciences and mathematics of the day. Modern philosophy owes far more to Newton than to capitalism. Moreover, there are ample grounds internal to the discipline to account for the development of current views from their classical sources. I am not a great fan of classical or modern empiricism. I find it hard to see, however, that it developed in response to anything beyond legitimate academic considerations.

These considerations hardly serve to refute Marxist claims. I hope, however, that they will persuade the reader to assess them with adequate suspicion.

This is by no means a complete view of academic freedom. I have only developed those features of the view that seemed to flow from the discussion of Part I. I have particularly not addressed questions concerning the scope of academic freedom – who is entitled to academic freedom, and what does it include? I shall conclude with some brief remarks on this topic.

Academic freedom as I have sketched it is intended to protect the process of inquiry. Inquiry is its heart and soul. It is not a civil right, nor is it a very general right. It paradigmatically applies to the faculty at universities engaged in research. And it applies primarily to their scholarly work. That includes their research and presumably also their teaching and service since these, in any good university, are part of the process of inquiry. Academic freedom is not, however, a general right of free speech and does not protect faculty when they speak, write or teach outside their areas of professional competence.

The doctrine of academic freedom applies to other institutions and contexts precisely to the degree that their members are engaged in the process of contributing to the growth of knowledge. I rather doubt if it is appropriate to the instruction of younger children. Much of early education is the simple transmission of basic skills and information – important, but hardly inquiry. Children should be encouraged to think, but doing so does not make the teacher into a scholar.

Lest this view of academic freedom seem overly narrow, it is important to remember that teachers in any context are entitled to a range of civil rights, including the right of free speech and press. Thus, when I claim that academic freedom does not protect the right of a chemistry professor to express views on politics and that academic freedom does not apply to the instructors of younger children, I do not mean to suggest that chemistry professors and elementary school teachers lack the right to express their views. Rather, the point is that such rights as they do have are more properly thought of as civil rights of the sort possessed by any citizen of a free country. That scholars teach, that teachers are often scholars, and that inquiry is often an important part of good teaching make it difficult clearly to mark the bounds of academic freedom. Nevertheless, academic freedom and the civil rights of free speech and press have different points. The character of each can be distorted by the conflation of them.

CHAPTER 6

# Student Rights

What rights do students have in educational institutions? How does the general framework of views on authority developed in Part I apply to those on the receiving end of education?

In order to took at the rights of students I want to begin by constructing a modest debate across the Atlantic and also across a bit more than a century. The question to be put is whether students and/or minors should have the same rights as adults? For the affirmative I shall briefly describe the views of the United States Supreme Court. For the negative, I shall state the position of John Stuart Mill. The dispute will, I believe, prove illuminating.

The United States Supreme Court was faced with the question of student rights when it received a case where students had been expelled from high school for wearing a black armband in protest at the United States involvement in the Viet Nam War. The opinion delivered by the Court in the case, *Tinker v. Des Moines*, extended a wide range of civil rights to students. In defending the right of students freely to express their political opinions in schools the Court made the following claims:

(1)   The wearing of an armband for the purpose of expressing a political opinion is a kind of symbolic speech and thus is protected by the provision of the United States Constitution that protects free speech.

(2)   People have whatever constitutional rights they have generally while they are in schools.

120

(3)  Students are legal persons and as a consequence have full constitutional rights.

These claims are intended by the Court to establish that the right of free speech is appropriately applied to students in the school context. That symbolic speech is constitutionally protected is not a novel point in American law. That minor children have full consitutional rights in schools is.

The Court added two more notable points:

(4)  Students have the right of free speech so long as they do not engage in conduct that materially and substantially disrupts the school's educational programme.
(5)  Free exchange of ideas is an important part of the educational process.

This last claim is of considerable interest for our inquiry. The Court believes that free expression has an important educational role. Two passages from the case will indicate the Court's view. Justice Fortas, writing for the Court and quoting Justice Jackson from another case, writes:

> That they are educating the young for citizenship is reason for scrupulous protection of Constitutional freedoms of the individual, if we are not to strangle the free mind at its source and teach youth to discount important principles of our government as mere platitudes.[1]

And quoting Justice Brennan:

> The classroom is peculiarly the 'marketplace of ideas.' The Nation's future depends upon leaders trained through wide exposure to that robust exchange of ideas which discovers truth 'out of a multitude of tongues' [rather] than through any kind of authoritative selection.[2]

These two passages can be expressed as two distinct arguments for extending the right of free speech to youth in school.

The first passage views the school as a model of the larger society. If schools are to train citizens for participation in a free society and if youth are not to see the principles of a free society as platitudes then the school must represent those principles faithfully. It must, in effect, practice what it preaches.

The second passage indicates that participation in the

process of a 'marketplace of ideas' is also an important component of learning the skills of citizenship in a democratic society. Students in a free society will live in an environment where decisions are thrashed out in vigorous public debate. They will need to learn to participate in such debates. The best way to learn the required skills is to participate in them in school.

It is most tempting to see the Court's argument as reflecting the kind of view of learning I argued in chapter 3. There I described the pedagogical relationship as akin to a master–apprentice relationship. Central features of being an apprentice are that one learns by modelling and by participation. Just what the Court has ordered. The student is seen as an apprentice citizen who learns by modelling and participating in the life of an institution that must faithfully reflect the political life of a free society if it is to do its job properly.

On reflection, however, this conclusion is not clearly warranted. It needs also to be remembered that in an apprenticeship relation there is a master who is distinguished from the novice by superior competence. This superior competence presumably conveys some right upon the master to organize and control the instructional process. Participation in a master–apprentice relationship is ordered and controlled by the master and is rooted in a presumption of inequality between the expert and the novice. The Court, however, has said that students are legal persons with full constitutional rights. They may be seen as having erected a presumption of equality between teacher and student so far as the right of free speech is concerned, and they may have weakened or eliminated the ability of the school to manage the 'marketplace of ideas' for educational purposes. It is thus not obvious that the Court's views are consistent with the position developed in chapter 3.

Note also that the understanding of the point of free speech exhibited in the Court's arguments reflects Mill's position in 'On Liberty'. Indeed, it is put in Mill's vocabulary. The school is a marketplace of ideas. Truth is pursued by a robust exchange of ideas and discovered out of a multitude of tongues. The Supreme Court has put much of Mill's views into the United States Constitution. It is, thus, surprising that Mill himself provides a significant line of argument against the view that the rights of minors should be the same as those of adults. Consider Mill's claims:

> ... This doctrine [of liberty] is meant to apply only to human beings in the maturity of their faculties. We are not speaking of children or of young persons below the age which the law may fix as that of manhood or womanhood. Those who are still in a state to require being taken care of by others must be protected against their own actions as well as against external inquiry.[3]

Mill points to two groups whom he regards as not in the maturity of their faculties – children and barbarians. Concerning the latter he notes:

> Despotism is a legitimate mode of government in dealing with barbarians, provided the end be their improvement and the means justified by actually effecting that end. Liberty, as a principle, has no application to the time when mankind have become capable of being improved by free and equal discussion.[4]

Mill does not provide an argument for these restrictions on liberty. One can, however, construct a quite reasonable one for him. Mill is a utilitarian. His defence of liberty depends on liberty promoting the general welfare. Liberty promotes the effective pursuit of truth, which in turn promotes the general welfare. I have already argued that I believe this to be a weak defence of civil liberties such as free speech. Here, however, the problem is slightly different. Even if Mill's argument is a satisfactory defence of such rights, it may be successful only for some groups of people. If we can identify persons where liberty is unlikely to promote inquiry and the general welfare, or if we can identify groups where liberty produces significant harmful effects, such that whatever advantage to the general welfare that results is outweighed by these effects, Mill's arguments for liberty will not justify liberty for these people. Children and other persons not in the maturity of their faculties presumably constitute such persons. The immature may harm themselves or others when given the same rights as adults. Moreover, the immature are unlikely to profit from free and equal discussion. The arguments Mill provides for liberty, arguments that depend on the consequences of liberty, do not succeed for the immature because liberty for the immature is unlikely to produce desirable consequences.

It thus appears that the US Supreme Court and John Stuart Mill would disagree concerning the rights of minors. Despite the fact that the Court relies heavily on Mill's view of the point of liberty, it appears to have little regard for his suggestion that liberty is not appropriate for those not in the maturity of their faculties.

Who is right? Before we begin to address this question, an additional point is required. Mill's concept of immaturity obscures a distinction that is of considerable interest in discussing the rights of students. It is important to distinguish between being immature and being a novice in some discipline. Although a person can be more immature about some things than about others, immaturity generally characterizes a person's overall capacity for sound judgement. It is not necessary to describe an individual as immature about this or that. One may be simply immature. Being a novice, however, is not a general condition. It is a specific state in relation to a specific kind of knowledge or competence. One cannot be simply a novice. One must be a novice in chemistry or carpentry. To be a novice is to lack skills or understanding of specific kinds in specific areas.

The extent to which being immature and being a novice are similar kinds of things is an open question. Perhaps being immature is being a novice about almost everything or about some very important things. I suspect, however, that more is involved. Being immature seems more than lacking intellectual skills of some sort. It is to lack other capacities, such as patience, self-control or restraint.

Clearly a person can be a novice about something and nevertheless be mature. The soundness of a person's judgement is not impugned by suggesting that he is ignorant of calculus. It also appears possible to be generally immature but quite expert in some particular subject.

This distinction is important in that if immaturity can be the basis of a suspension or reduction of rights, such reductions may prove to be broad in their scope, touching every area of a person's life. If, however, being a novice can be the basis of a suspension or reduction of rights, any such loss will be confined to a particular context.

I have also argued that it is important to distinguish arguments for academic freedom and, more generally, arguments concerned with inquiry and learning, from arguments for civil rights such as free speech. Academic freedom and free speech have different points and different justifications. Being a novice is a condition that pertains to intellectual or educational contexts. If being a novice is pertinent to having or not having rights, the rights it will be pertinent to will be those of academic freedom. Being immature, however, may provide grounds for denying a person a wide range of civil rights. It can be held to be relevant to any right that requires sound judgement for its competent exercise. The distinction between being a novice and being immature is, therefore, important if we are to avoid confusing academic freedom with more general civil liberties. We need also, however, to keep in mind that both kinds of rights and, therefore, both being immature and being a novice pertain to the question of liberty in education.

I shall first take up the question of whether immaturity can provide a justification for distinguishing the rights of the immature and the mature. It will be helpful here to think of the issue as the justification of paternalism. To say that the immature have fewer or different rights than others is to say that others may direct their lives in areas where such direction would normally be impermissible.

I shall argue that the rights of 'those not in the maturity of their faculties' differ from the rights of mature adults. However, Mill's arguments will not suffice to show this, since I have rejected the view about rights that they presuppose. I have argued that civil rights are not primarily rooted in considerations of the kinds of institutions that promote the average welfare. Rather, they are rooted in what it means to be a person. The 'intellectual liberties' such as free speech are justified by the fact that persons are moral agents who are responsible for their own choices and their own actions. They thus have the right not to be unreasonably interfered with in their choices and the right to institutions that make competent choice possible. Liberties such as freedom of religion, speech, press and assembly are included among these institutions.

*The problem is that there is a sense in which those not in the maturity of their faculties are not moral agents.* This point is best made by examining an extreme case. Consider then the status of an infant or small child. Infants are certainly persons and have some of the rights of persons. They are proper objects of respect and are ends in themsleves. They may not be treated as pure instrumentalities. And they are moral agents in the sense that they belong to the class of beings who can make moral choices. But the infant's capacity to make morally responsible choices is largely an unactualized potential. In this regard small children are not moral agents. They are not capable of making choices on moral grounds, and they are not capable of judging the consequences of their actions. It is not that small children are immoral or often act negligently. These are perversions of moral judgement, which assume that the individual possesses the actualized capacity for sound judgement but declines to use it. The infant, however, simply lacks the capacity.

This lack is most clearly exhibited in that we characteristically are unwilling to treat small children as responsible for their actions. When a small child breaks something, writes on the wall or hurts another child, we may punish the child or seek to prevent further occurrences. But, if we are thinking about it at all, we do not hold the child to be morally culpable. For doing so requires the assumption that the child is able to judge the consequences of his acts, evaluate them on appropriate moral criteria, and to control his behaviour in light of such considerations. Children are often lacking on all of these grounds. They are not, thus, moral agents, in the sense that they lack the requisite capacities of moral agency.

Note that these remarks contain an implicit conception of the components of moral agency. One component of moral agency is the ability to know what one is doing. This involves being able to judge the consequences of one's actions, but it has a broader meaning. It is also the ability to assign a public meaning to one's actions and to judge their human significance. One must be able, for example, to see some acts as offensive, evil or ill-mannered and others as kind or proper. The second component of moral agency is the capacity to apply appropriate moral standards to judging actions. One must have some understanding of what counts as just, fair or moral and must be able to use this understanding to deliberate about and judge actions. The final component of moral agency is the ability to regulate one's behaviour in accordance with the above sorts of deliberations, i.e., self-control. A person who is unable to act on the basis of appropriate deliberations even though he can engage in them is not fully a moral agent.

The way of not being in the maturity of one's faculties that is relevant to my argument is to be lacking in one or more of these components of moral agency. Why should immaturity in this sense be a reason to restrict a person's rights or be the justification of paternalism? I can suggest three reasons why this should be the case.

Most important is that it is the point of many liberties to protect the exercise of moral agency. It is because people are responsible for themselves that they have a right to choose for themselves and act on their choices. And it is because they must have the means for competent choice that they have a right to a society in which ideas and information can be freely shared. These rights, however, assume the fact of moral agency. They are intended to permit its expression. Where people have not actualized their capacity for moral agency, these rights do not serve their point.

The morally immature also fail to understand the significance of their acts. It is important to note here that failing to understand the significance of one's acts is a broader notion than failing to understand the consequences of one's acts. There are numerous cases where children know what the consequences of what they do will be, but do not fully understand the significance of those consequences. Children often tease one another. They know quite well that hurt feelings can result. That is often why they do it. But they often fail to understand the moral seriousness of wilfully causing hurt to another. Likewise teenagers usually know that sex can lead to pregnancy. They often fail, however, to understand the significance and responsibilities of creating human life or of terminating it capriciously. I have emphasized this distinction between knowing the consequences and knowing the significances of one's actions because I believe that not attending to it easily leads to a trivialization of the harm that the immature can unwittingly do to themselves and others. Those who focus on the consequences of actions may be persuaded to agree that very small children should be prevented from playing with matches. But they are also likely to be impressed with the fact that children of 8 to 10 years often have quite reasonable notions of the physical consequences of what they do. They are, as a result, likely to overestimate the maturity of children. But older children who know the consequences of their acts may, nonetheless, badly misjudge their own interest or enter into relations or commitments with little grasp of their full meaning. They may thereby do serious, but subtle, damage to themselves and others. The primary point of paternalism is not to protect small children from doing physical harm to themselves, although it is that. It is, rather, to prevent the immature from making choices, taking on commitments and relationships, or choosing directions for their lives when they cannot grasp their significance.

The final reason why immaturity provides reasonable grounds for restricting rights and for paternalism is that participation in a system of rights by large numbers of persons who do not understand their point or cannot use them effectively can damage the usefulness of rights for everyone. Consider, for example, voting. Voting may be understood as a social mechanism that records and balances competing interests. People have a right to determine what is good for them and to pursue such interests as they choose. When interests conflict, a just mechanism for adjudicating and balancing interests is required. Voting arguably does this. A candidate, in order to secure election, will have to appeal to the widest possible range of interests. Voters, in turn, select candidates by identifying their interests and matching them to the views of candidates. In such a way people who represent the broadest range of interests will succeed and the process of collective decision-making will be legitimate. So, at least, goes the theory.

However, such a process will succeed only if the majority of those who participate in it understand their interests and have reasonable views concerning the policies that promote their interests. If large numbers of people vote who do not have reasonable views of their interests or the policies that promote them, the electoral process will begin to produce irrational results and will cease to be a means whereby people can successfully aggregate their interests. Moreover, the electoral process will fail for everyone, not just for those who do not use it intelligently. Elections, like most democratic institutions, cannot tolerate an excess of stupidity.

A similar point can be made for free speech. The free exchange of ideas is likely to be productive socially and individually only so long as most of those who participate in the process do so with a modicum of intelligence. Otherwise, the marketplace of ideas will degenerate into a Babel of confusion. Intellectual forums are sensitive not only to censorships, but to 'noise'.

The capacity of free institutions to tolerate participation by the immature is not, therefore, infinite. It may not even be substantial. Such considerations also provide grounds for paternalism and limiting the rights of the immature.

It should not be overlooked that these arguments can easily be turned to the justification of substantial abuses. Who, after all, are the immature? How shall they be identified? Who shall decide about them? Arguments of the sort I have given above have historically been used to justify slavery, oppression of other nations and peoples, and the denial of civil rights to women and minorities. It is worth remembering that Mill, who is hardly timid in his defence of liberty, nevertheless included 'barbarians' among those not in the maturity of their faculties.

That such arguments are readily abused is a compelling reason for caution in how they are applied, but is not a reason for ignoring their force. Some general criteria for their application are, therefore, in order. The first thing to keep in mind is that maturity is a matter of degree. It is not something one either has or does not have. Moreover, most human beings acquire it gradually and informally over a period of years. Also, being in the maturity of one's faculties does not require any great knowledge or intellectual sophistication. Maturity is, rather, the ability to understand the meaning of routine everyday actions, the ability to judge them according to moral standards and the ability to control one's actions. These are abilities possessed by the vast majority of adult human beings, although some may be more sophisticated in such matters than others. Failure to possess these qualities is not a consequence of lack of intellectual sophistication or training. Failure is pathological.

These points suggest that a strong presumption exists that adults possess the prerequisite maturity to entitle them to full civil rights. This is a presumption that needs to be rebutted if an adult is to be denied any liberty. However, it would not be rebutted by showing, for example, that the individual was not especially bright or that his choices often went wrong. It could be rebutted only by showing that the person was incapable of judging the meaning of his actions or of regulating his own behaviour. Thus, the rebuttal of the presumption of maturity requires a demonstration of pathology. With the exception of the mentally ill or senile, all adults are in the maturity of their faculties.

The discussion also suggests that the capacities involved in maturity admit of high levels of development and that there can be vast degrees of difference in sophistication in them. One need not, for example, be trained in moral philosophy to be able to judge human activities in moral terms. Normal people do this routinely. Training in moral philosophy may, however, add considerable sophistication and depth to one's moral judgements and reflections. It does not follow, therefore, because adults are routinely mature, that the components of maturity cannot be refined or that education is unimportant for their refinement. Quite the opposite is the case.

Finally, with respect to maturity, children differ from adults in two important ways: immaturity is not a pathology, and immaturity is the normal state of affairs. Children are simply born without the capacities that comprise maturity. These capacities are acquisitions, achievements. Lacking them in a child is merely a function of being a child. It is not pathological. There is, thus, a presumption in favour of the view that a child is immature and is an appropriate object of paternalism.

That children are proper objects of paternalism does not, of course, entitle any adult to order about any child as whim strikes. There must be some rights and duties attached to a paternalistic relationship. Moreover, we shall need to know who is entitled to be paternal towards whom. I shall defer the second question to the next chapter. Here we need to attend to the issue of the rights and duties attached to the paternalistic relationship.

The particular form of this issue that we need to address concerns the character of paternalism between adult and child. (The character of paternalism when the need for paternalism is rooted in a pathology is presumbly different.)

The most important point to make about the paternalistic

relationship is that *there is a general duty for the adult who controls some part of the life of a child to act for the sake of the interests and well-being of the child.* We can understand this general duty better by recalling the force of the justification of paternalism. The child is a person. That entitles the child to the respect due to any human being – to be treated as an end, not as a means. But the child is also a person whose human potentials are substantially unactualized. That is what makes the child a proper object of paternalism. It seems reasonable in this light to suggest that the fundamental duty owed to a child in the paternalistic relationship is to help the child to actualize those human potentials, the possession of which makes one an autonomous moral agent entitled to the full range of human rights and the lack of which subjects the child to paternalism.

This is a correct, but incomplete, view. Every person, children included, has legitimate interests that it is his right to pursue. To regard an individual as a person – someone who is an end, not a means – is to give a *prima facie* validity to that person's interests. That I am a person and that I want something is not a sufficient reason why I should have it, but it is *a* reason why I should have it. Since children are also persons, it follows that they also have the right to have their interests granted *prima facie* validity. Thus, when someone who is responsible for the well-being of a child chooses on behalf of a child, that person has a duty to choose in ways that promote the child's interests.

Identifying a child's interests is, however, a difficult matter. One of the privileges accorded an adult is the presumption that the interests of an adult are what the adult believes them to be. We may disagree with some adult about what his interests really are, but we are not entitled to impose our view of his interests on him. Being the author of one's own sense of one's good is a right accorded to moral agents.

It is a different matter for children, however. The arguments for paternalism indicate that children are not the best judge of their interests, nor are they entitled to be the judge of their interests. Children require an adult to help them decide on their interests and occasionally to choose for them in ways consistent with their *real* interests. A child's interests may differ notably from what the child thinks them to be.

How shall we decide what a child's real interests are? Here I

shall proceed by suggesting some broad and somewhat over-
lapping classes of interests. They should give a reasonable
indication of the duties adults owe to children to whom they
stand in a paternalistic relationship.

First, and most obvious, the *child has an interest in nurture*. I
would include here such things as safety, security, protection,
love and care for basic physical and emotional needs. These are
things that everyone needs, but they are peculiarly things for
which children depend on adults.

Second, *the child has an interest in acquiring the prerequisites of
moral agency, personal autonomy and independence*. This is to
say, at least, that children have an interest in actualizing those
potentials that characterize mature adults. They need to
understand the significance of their actions in appropriate ways,
and they need to be able to apply appropriate moral concepts to
the evaluation of their acts and their goals. They also need a
sufficient sense of their own worth and sufficient mental health
to be able to feel entitled to act in their own interest and to take
responsibility for their own behaviour. It is also important to
keep in mind that autonomy has not only cognitive and
emotional prerequisites, but material ones as well. Children are
thus entitled to the opportunity to become economically self-
supporting and to acquire competencies that make that
possible.

These kinds of interests are the interests of every person. They
impose duties on the adults who have the responsibility to care
for children that are in that sense uniform. It may be that these
interests can be met in different ways for different children, but
all children have them and are entitled so far as possible to have
adults act towards them so as to fulfil these interests.

There is, however, a final class of interests that will be the
interests of particular children. These are numerous personal
goals and pursuits in which particular children can have an
interest. *All people, for example, need to develop some set of
personal preferences or tastes in areas such as music, food, dress,
occupation or recreation. Acquiring such a set of preferences is
part of becoming a person.* People need a set of personal goods
that they make their goods. There are few universals in such
matters. Not everyone need like Bach or basketball. Nevertheless, the choice of the direction one's preferences will take is a

matter in which one can be wrong. A given preference can be something ill-suited to one's talents or character. It can require resources beyond one's means or have unknown consequences. Moreover, children are particularly liable to mistakes in such preferences. They are likely to be responsive to the superficial aspects of an activity, rather than its more subtle and enduring, but less accessible, features, and they often lack insight into their own character and capacities.

Helping children to develop a reasonable sense of the kinds of preferences and talents they should acquire and the kinds of goods they should pursue is a most difficult matter. While children are often in a poor position to judge such matters, these are not easily judged by adults for children either. Moreover, it is often impossible as well as undesirable to compel a preference. Nothing is more likely to diminish interest in some activity than being compelled to pursue it. On the other hand, it is an abdication of the responsibilities of parents and teachers to fail to provide guidance with respect to the preferences children acquire. Surely there is a duty to help children learn to enjoy some of those things that human experience has shown to be of enduring value and to help them avoid those things that are ephemeral or destructive. And there is a duty to help children pursue activities that fit their talents and character. Compulsion here is rarely necessary. What is required is guidance and structured opportunity, provided with wisdom and insight into the child's particular needs.

These arguments concerning paternalism support several conclusions. Initially, they indicate that *the proposition that the civil rights of children should be coextensive with those of adults is untenable. Paternalism is a reasonable institution toward the immature*, despite the fact that, by definition, it involves restrictions on children that would be impermissible if applied to adults.

The arguments also indicate that *those adults entitled to paternalistic authority over children owe them a set of duties of three sorts. Children are entitled to nurture, the prerequisites of moral agency, autonomy and independence, and the resources and guidance that will help them to acquire a set of rational preferences and develop their own unique potential.* These duties toward children obviously imply some things about education. *The last two types of duties indicate a need for education that is liberating and humanizing in the broadest sense.*

Here, however, it is also important to note what does not follow from these arguments. It does not follow that schools are entitled to exercise paternalistic authority over students – for two reasons. First, the arguments do not apply at all to mature students. The college student, for example, is presumed to be in the maturity of his faculties. College students are not, thus, proper objects of paternalism. They are entitled to the same range of civil rights as any adult. Moreover, if in their role of student or novice, students have fewer privileges or rights than teachers or experts, that will have to be justified in ways that differ from the arguments for paternalism and will have to be limited to the student role. That a college student knows little about chemistry may be a reason for putting him in a subservient position to a professor or lecturer in a chemistry class, but it is not a reason for restricting his civil rights.

The second difficulty in applying the arguments for paternalism to schools is that, where children are concerned, it is one thing to show that they are proper objects of paternalism. It is quite another to show that it is schools that are entitled to exercise paternalistic authority. Most Western societies begin with the presumption that it is parents who are responsible for their children and who are entitled to paternalistic authority over them. If so, we should have to give an account of how the authority of parents gets to be exercised by schools.

It is worth noting here that if the school is entitled to exercise some of the authority of parents over children, the child may stand in a kind of double jeopardy before the authority of the school. For the child in school is both a novice in the areas of learning that schools promote and an immature person. The school will, then, exercise both the authority of the expert over the novice and the authority of the parent over the child.

We now need to focus on the role of the student. The argument thus far has suggested that children should not have the same civil rights as adults. Perhaps, however, this is a bit unfair to the argument given by the US Supreme Court. They were not, after all, arguing that parents are not entitled to exercise authority over their children. They were defending the claim that students have the right of free speech in schools. Moreover, they defended this in terms of specific educational arguments concerning the importance of the 'marketplace of ideas' in learning. Perhaps, then, we can defend the Supreme Court against Mill by focusing more particularly on the role of students in schools.

Curiously, we might even bring Mill to the aid of the Supreme Court in this matter. The reader will recall that I argued in Part I that one aim of instruction in any area of thought is to bring the student into a position of intellectual independence in that area. It is to move the novice in the direction of the expert. I have just finished arguing an analogous, but broader, claim concerning paternalism. One of the duties owed to children is to allow them to achieve those competencies that are the prerequisites of mature judgement and personal autonomy. But how is such maturity achieved? The Supreme Court sees the marketplace of ideas as central in the instruction of youth for participation in a free society. Mill expresses an analogous sentiment.

> He who lets the world, or his own portion of it, choose his plan of life for him has no need of any other faculty than the age-old one of imitation. He who chooses his plan for himself employs all his faculties. He must use observation to see, reasoning and judgement to foresee, activity to gather materials for decision, firmness, and self-control to hold to his deliberate decision. And these qualities he requires and exercises exactly in proportion as the part of his conduct which he determines according to his judgement and feeling is a large one.[5]

Mill's formulation of this argument is stated in terms of a dated psychology. He appears to see the development of personal and intellectual talent as rather like exercising a muscle. So far as intellectual competence is concerned, this is surely odd, for it appears to divorce the idea of intellectual growth from learning the concepts and criteria that govern an area of thought. Nevertheless, Mill's basic idea is sound. Growth in any skill requires participation and practice. People do not normally acquire capacities they have no occasion to employ. Moreover, it is difficult to see that a person would have the chance to employ those capacities that enable people to assume competent control over their lives unless they had the freedom to decide for themselves. People who lack freedom have no need to be able to decide for themselves. Freedom promotes personal competence. Authority precludes it.

The US Supreme Court's argument seems merely a variant on this theme. If we expect students to acquire the competencies appropriate to free people living in democratic societies, students must be free in schools. Students will not learn how to participate in a marketplace of ideas if the school is a cartel of authoritarianism. Perhaps, then, the Supreme Court's arguments are quite defensible as a view of schooling.

In considering such claims, it will be helpful to distinguish between the curricular and the extra-curricular components of schooling. Those activities that are the centre of the official curriculum, activities such as mathematics, science or language, can be seen as having a peculiarly academic cast to them. They are intended to transmit some theoretical forms of knowledge. Other activities, whether they are officially part of the school's extra-curricular programme, such as sports, or simply the informal interaction of students, are less clearly academic in their character. They do, however, play a role in education, which is perhaps distinguishable from the role of the normal academic curriculum.

Concerning the character of rights in the classroom, we first have to state the question more sharply. In Part I, I argued that there were reasons for distinguishing between the rights and duties of novices and experts. That discussion is certainly relevant to the issue at hand. However, we must be careful not to assume that the expert/novice distinction is sufficient here. In a classroom, not every adult is an expert and not every novice is a child. Moreover, one must not assume that all rights are at issue. I have argued that academic freedom is distinct from general civil rights. Perhaps only academic freedom is at issue in the classroom.

The best way to proceed is to recall what was said earlier concerning the relation between novice and expert and to see what qualifications to that view are required. The view previously developed saw the relationship between expert and novice as a master–apprentice relationship. The student is a junior member of an intellectual community united by a commitment to some commonly understood intellectual enterprise. Learning occurs by participation by the novice in the characteristic enterprises of the group under the direction of an expert who will set tasks and evaluate performance.

This view suggests some features that are quite compatible with the arguments given for student rights. Learning involves participation. The notion that learning requires doing the thing one is learning about is an essential part of the Supreme Court's argument and of mine. But there the difference ends. I do not conclude that the classroom must be a marketplace of ideas. *The classroom is not primarily a place where truth is discovered out of the debates and conversations of equals. It is a place where a novice attempts to understand and acquire the concepts, standards and procedures of a way of thinking under the direction of an expert.* Participation may be a part of learning here, and participation may well include arguments and debates. It is hard, for example, to imagine learning philosophy in a way that did not involve philosophical arguing. This kind of participation does not, however, convey equal status on the novice and the expert. It does not 'liberate' the student from the guidance of the teacher. Indeed, it does not convey rights upon the student. *In the master–apprentice relationship, participation is something organized by the master for the apprentice. It is not a right held by the apprentice against the authority of the master.* Such a way of viewing it misrepresents the character of the roles involved and seems a perversion of a relationship that must rest, in the final analysis, on trust and respect.

But not every student is a child and there are rights that fall outside the master–apprentice relationship. Being an adult conveys on one the full array of civil rights. For our concerns this has two implications. First, it implies that, *for an adult, acceptance of the role of a novice and the kind of subservience implied must be voluntary.* The teacher has only the power to say 'if you wish to learn chemistry, you must submit to my guidance and direction in the matter, otherwise I cannot teach it to you'. That does not, however, involve the power to compel anyone to learn chemistry. Nor does it involve the waiving of any civil rights – rights that are the privilege of all adults and that are unrelated to learning chemistry. The second implication is that, although *the adult student in a chemistry class is not the equal of the chemist in chemistry, as a citizen, he is the equal of the chemist and possesses the same rights. It is, thus, improper to narrow the scope of the rights of the adult student beyond the needs or context of instruction.*

The child in a classroom, however, is both a novice and a child. The teacher, insofar as he is entitled to paternal authority, may well exercise authority over the child beyond what is required by the particular subject matter at issue. Perhaps the child may be compelled to study some subject because it is seen by the teacher to be in the child's best interest to study it. And the teacher may be entitled to interfere in the child's plans and choices in ways that are not related to instruction in some subject matter, but that are more broadly concerned with the child's welfare and growth.

The matter becomes more complex when we begin to ask about student rights in activities beyond the official curriculum. The first question to focus on is raised by the ambiguity of the notion of things that are not part of the official curriculum. This can cover a wide variety of enterprises, from clubs to musical groups, to sports, to dormitory life. Here I wish to focus on political activity and particularly on the expression of political views. Such activities are usually the focal point of controversy. Moreover, despite the fact that such activities are extra-curricular, they serve an educational function. This is testified to by the fact that educational officials often seek to initiate them or support them. Many secondary schools and universities, for example, will have student newspapers that are commonly initiated by and subsidized by the institution, even though they are run by students. These papers often provide forums for the expression of political views.

Because participation in political activities of various sorts has an educational point, it might be argued that the fact that it is extra-curricular is incidental. Why not treat political activity as we would science or mathematics? The student writing an editorial on some matter of controversy for the student paper is not, in principle, different from the student working on math problems or doing an experiment in science class. Just as students can be novice chemists or mathematicians, they can be novice journalists or political scientists. Such an argument has the consequence that experts are entitled to exercise control over the forms of political activity and expression that occur in educational contexts. They would be entitled to set tasks and evaluate results. Generally, they would be entitled to regulate the political activities and expression of students for educational purposes.

This conclusion, however, is not acceptable. To accept it is to misconstrue the character of political knowledge and the point of political discussion. The normal concepts of political discourse are more accessible, less esoteric and less organized into tight conceptual systems than are the concepts of physics. This implies that they are not legitimately treated as the exclusive property of some intellectual guild. The authority of experts over such concepts is questionable.

I have also argued that the point of free and open debates about political concepts has a different function from free and open debate concerning academic issues. In the latter case, the point is to add to the store of human knowledge or, in the case of a novice, to internalize the standards and procedures of a field. Free and open discussion provides the resources for competent individual choice and provides for the opportunity to participate in collective choice. Since political participation is not directed primarily to the advancement of the goals of a discipline, it again seems inappropriate to assimilate it to the forms of intellectual authority rooted in such purposes. This, too, is a reason for not extending the kind of authority appropriate to the expert–novice relationship to the context of political activities and expression.

It does not follow, however, that political activity and expression do not perform an educational role. Competent and effective involvement in such matters is clearly learned. Moreover, it is quite reasonable to suppose that the skills involved in political activities and expression, like other complex skills, are learned by participation and practice.

In this set of remarks, we have the makings of a reasonable case that the educational views of the US Supreme Court make excellent sense when applied to such extra-curricular activities as political activities and expression. It seems that learning to perform these activities competently does involve participation and practice. And it seems that the elitist view of authority appropriate to the standard curriculum is inappropriate to such activities. Such considerations indicate that there are good educational reasons for protecting those civil rights of students that concern political activity and expression. Rights such as free speech, free press and freedom of association play an important educational role. Perhaps, then, we can conclude that in such areas students should have the same rights as adults.

Two further questions need to be addressed before we can safely draw such a conclusion. The arguments that indicate that protecting the rights of students has beneficial consequences are empirical arguments. It is, therefore, worth asking whether or not there is any evidence to confirm the claim that protecting such rights for students does have desirable consequences. Second, the argument to this point has not yet addressed the issue of paternalism. Concerning rights such as free speech or press, are there any reasons to suppose that minor students should have fewer rights than adult students, or than adults in general?

*Civil rights, such as free speech and free press, presumably can be seen as serving two broad functions. They can secure the right of individuals to participate in collective decisions, and they can protect minorities from oppression by the majority.*

Individuals and groups may differ significantly concerning which of these two functions of rights they most value. People who feel themselves to be full participants in their societies are not likely to feel the need of protection from the majority's values and decisions. Often they will feel themselves to be the majority and that the majority's values are their values. They will, however, desire to participate in collective judgements. Thus, they will value rights because rights secure the privilege of participation.

Individuals and groups who do *not* see themselves as belonging to a society's mainstream may also value rights because they help secure the opportunity to be heard and to participate in a society's affairs. Indeed, the opportunity for such participation may be far more important to these people because the majority may otherwise ignore their concerns. It may be, however, that some groups, particularly groups who have little desire to join the mainstream of a society, will attach far more value to the protection that rights afford them than to the opportunity to participate. Groups with distinctive and divergent religions, ideologies or cultures may seek little more from the majority than to be left in peace to practise their own convictions. In such cases, people will not be especially interested in debating their views with others in some cultural marketplace of ideas. Rather, they will be most interested in sharing with each other, developing a common culture and being left alone to do so. The best examples of such groups are religious minorities, such as the Amish, who consciously seek isolation from the cultures in which they are located and the freedom to live in their own way. It will, however, inevitably be true to a degree of any group that sees itself as culturally distinct from the majority.

These points can be captured in the following generalization: *in-groups, those that see themselves as belonging to the majority culture, will value rights primarily because rights secure participation. Out-groups, however, will value rights primarily because they provide defence against the values of the dominant culture.*

This point is important to the question of student rights because there is reason to believe that many students see themselves as members of an out-group and have an out-group's view of rights. One of the consequences of schooling in advanced industrial societies is that students are excluded from full participation in their society until they near their twenties. In fact, much of adult life is invisible to students. Moreover, schools are structured in a way that students are in contact primarily with other individuals of their own age. Arguably, then, schools diminish the influence of adults and adult values on youth, and enhance the influence of peers. The result is that students, to a degree, see themselves as a distinct class with distinct values and interests.

A recent report of the Panel on Youth of the President's Science Advisory Committee in the USA describes the consequences:

The political repercussions to society of keeping a large and able fraction of its members as outsiders, with no history or experience of responsibility, until well after they are politically active, are certainly great. It creates a special political bias, in which many of the most able members of future elites become politically active while still in an outsider's status, still able to view the world only from the position of an outsider. It creates a warm-hearted, sympathetic, and open political stance, one which focuses on certain principles like equal opportunity and civil rights, but ignores others, such as honesty, reward for merit, and the rule of law.[6]

A colleague and I have produced some evidence that this sense of being an outsider infects the student's view of his own civil rights. We have given a survey to about 700 high school students in New York concerning student rights. Consider the response on five of the items shown in the table.

TABLE 1    STUDENTS' VIEWS OF STUDENT RIGHTS

|  |  | Agree | Disagree | Undecided |
|---|---|---|---|---|
| (1) | The rights of freedom of speech and freedom of press should protect the right to criticize persons in positions of authority, such as senators or mayors. | 94 | 2 | 4 |
| (2) | The free speech of a student should give him or her the right to be critical of school authorities. | 66 | 17 | 17 |
| (3) | A school should be able to limit a student's expression of opinion if what he or she says is in favour of communism or some other radical doctrine. | 17 | 60 | 23 |
| (4) | The faculty advisor for a student paper permitted students to print remarks critical of others only when these remarks were backed up with facts. Do you agree with this policy? | 59 | 27 | 14 |
| (5) | A student's expression of opinion may be limited when what is said might hurt someone's feelings. | 66 | 22 | 17 |

The first item contains no mention of who is doing the criticism, although the students we interviewed usually assumed that it was students. The objects of criticism are remote persons – senators or mayors. Students are virtually unanimous in agreeing that criticism of such persons should be protected. The second item differs from the first primarily in that the person criticized is a local person – someone in the student's life. Students are generally willing to permit criticism of such local adults, but they are far from unanimous about it. Generally, however, students believe quite strongly that they are entitled to criticize adults. The third item involves a situation where adults are seen as patronizing students concerning their political ideas. There were other items on the questionnaire that represented adults as protecting students from pornographic material. Students generally believe that adults should not be entitled to protect them from radical ideas or obscene material. The last two items represent adults as intervening to prevent criticism of one student by another. Item 4 was intended by us to be concerned with unproven allegations. Our evidence suggests, however, that what students are responding to is implied criticism of one student by another. This is clearly what is meant by the fifth item. Students are quite accepting of adult intervention in such cases.

It seems most reasonable to interpret these responses as the result of an out-group's view of the rights involved. Two factors seem involved. On the one hand, students believe that they are entitled to criticize others without interference when those others are remote adults. They are most willing to have their speech interfered with when the objects of criticism are their immediate peers. The point is not that they are strongly convinced that they are entitled to criticize public officials but not one another. Rather, their responses seem dominated by a sense that remote adults are just that – remote adults. Students have little feeling for these persons or their roles. Why should they not be criticized? They are fair game because they are outside the student's range of concerns. Peers, however, are not similarly distant. The student must continue to live in the same world with these potential targets, so there is concern for their feelings. Indeed, for those students we interviewed, peer relations were most important. Yet they were seen as most fragile, fragile enough that students appeared quite willing to permit adults to intervene when they were threatened.

Adult intervention in the affairs of students is far less welcome when students perceive it as a matter of adults imposing their views on students. Students thus have little patience with adults who wish to protect them from dangerous or immoral ideas. Communism and pornography are perceived as adult hang-ups.

These results suggest that *the values students attach to rights are much influenced by their sense of themselves as a distinct group with its own values and concerns.* They attach little value to rights so far as participation in the decisions of adults is concerned. No doubt they are simply being reasonable. For the most part, they do not identify with adult debates and have little desire to participate in them. They do, however, value rights when those rights serve to protect them from what they see as adult encroachment or imposition. Moreover, they are first and foremost concerned with their peers. This concern is reflected both in their desire to keep adults at a distance when peer values are threatened and in their willingness to allow adults to intervene in potentially unpleasant situations, even if such intervention violates their rights.

That students tend to see themselves as an out-group and have an out-group view of rights has considerable bearing on the educational consequences of student rights. The US Supreme Court appears to claim that schools are to function as models of a free society and that students are to learn how to function in such a society through participation in a market-place of ideas in schools. That students see themselves as members of an out-group, however, raises serious questions about whether students are likely to learn the intended lessons. *The Court wishes to see students as apprentice participants in a democratic form of government. Students may not share the vision. To the extent that they do not, they are unlikely to benefit from participation in the marketplace of ideas.*

Perhaps more serious is the possibility that an emphasis on student rights may serve to legitimate to students their sense of cultural independence from the adult world. What students may learn is that they are entitled to their own values and beliefs. That is a difficult conclusion. I suspect that most readers of this volume will be pleased that adults are not entitled to restrict the ideas that students may encounter. I am, also. But one must also remember that the essence of education is the transmission of a cultural heritage from one generation to another. If the adult 'hang-ups' students wish to be liberated from are a love of learning, and appreciation of art, science, music or mathematics, we must be less than enthusiastic about conveying any message that legitimates a rejection of adult values.

I am much afraid that this is what students will, in fact, learn from an emphasis on student rights. If the major consequence of talk about student rights is that students believe themselves entitled to avoid the education adults seek to provide, student rights is a less than felicitous topic. We should recall that education is dependent on trust and respect between teacher and learner. The need to talk about rights, however, is an indication of widespread estrangement. It is, thus, a symptom of a larger disease. Perhaps, then, the proper response to the question of student rights is not so much to try to work out a detailed position on what rights students ought to have. It is, rather, to look to the roots of intergenerational estrangement and to try to find ways to make youth into genuine participants in adult life. The basis of youth's sense of being an out-group is that youth are an out-group. The difficulty with the Supreme Court's arguments is that this out-group status will not appreciably change by waving the Constitution at it. This is not to say that students ought not to have rights. It is only to suggest that the arguments of the US Supreme Court, arguments that claim desirable educational consequences for student rights, are not convincing.

Let us consider another approach. The Supreme Court is attempting to provide a positive justification for student rights. The presumption seems to be that some such justification is required. We might also start with the presumption that students have rights and ask if there are any considerations that can rebut it. I can think of four reasons that might be held to rebut the presumption that students have rights:

(1) Students are immature and may exercise their rights in ways that unnecessarily cause harm to themselves and others.

(2) Students are immature and need to be protected from some ideas or some kinds of influence because they lack the maturity or judgement to deal with them in a reasonable manner.

(3) Students need guidance in learning how to exercise their rights competently and responsibly. Adults may thus

intervene in a student's exercise of some right to the extent
that there is a legitimate educational reason for doing so.
(4)   Some ideas are false or inherently offensive and should not
      be permitted to be introduced into an educational
      situation.

The first three arguments are linked to the presumed immaturity of students. They thus raise the issue as to whether
paternalism towards minors can be extended to basic civil
rights. I see nothing *a priori* problematic with such arguments.
Students may, in fact, do harm by what they write or say. I know
of several local instances where ill-conceived attempts by
students to publish humorous caricatures of other students in
school newspapers caused substantial psychological harm. In a
society that believes in a free press, such acts, when they involve
adults, are dealt with by libel laws, not censorship or prior
constraint. Such solutions seem inappropriate for the immature. They punish the offence, rather than prevent it, and
they assume that the perpetrators are fully responsible for their
conduct and understand the meaning of their actions. Students
often lack a full grasp of the human significance of derisive
treatment of one another. It is something they need to learn.
Adults can teach the lesson and prevent the damage, but they
can only do so if they are entitled to intervene in the student's
expression of views.

The defect in such arguments is that they are easily abused.
This is particularly true of the second one. While in principle it is
possible that there are ideas or influences that immature
students should be protected from, in most cases when this sort
of argument is made, it turns out to be a pretext to prevent
students from encountering an idea with which some adult
disagrees. Such arguments become euphemisms for censorship.

Indeed, in the vast majority of student rights cases, it is an
argument of the fourth type that is involved. This seems clearly
the case in *Tinker v. Des Moines*, the case in which the Supreme
Court develops its views. Behind all the debate is the obvious
fact that students were expressing their rejection of the United
States' military involvement in Viet Nam and that school
officials found that to be unpatriotic and offensive.

I want to insist that arguments of the fourth sort are never acceptable. When the expression of a point of view is rejected simply because of distaste for the idea expressed, the act of rejection displays contempt both for the process of rational deliberation and for the right of individuals to make autonomous choices. Morever, *when an adult represses the opinion of a child simply because he believes that opinion to be wrong, the adult is treating the child as a means to his own ends, rather than as an object of intrinsic worth. Arguments of the fourth sort thus involve a rejection of the basic values of a free society.* All of the arguments heretofore advanced in defence of a free society weigh against them. That students may be immature makes no difference here, for the concern is not to advance the understanding of an immature person or to protect him from harm. Rather, the concern is to deny someone the opportunity to assess and choose an unpopular idea. *Respect for students as persons excludes gratuitous restrictions on their liberty.*

*The essence, then, of the argument for student rights is simply that in a free society school officials should not be permitted to act in ways that express contempt for the values of a free society.* They must not be permitted to act as though they are entitled to be the author of another person's views, and they must not be permitted to act as though their assessment of the worth of an idea were sufficient to eliminate the need for critical assessment by others. Finally, they must not be permitted to show contempt for the worth and dignity of their students.

*The primary point of expecting school officials to act in ways consistent with the values of a free society is that these values are important and should be affirmed.* That such actions have beneficial educational consequences is to be earnestly desired, but it is not altogether crucial to the argument. Suppose it could be shown that the best way to assure that students come to appreciate the values of a free society was to oppress them relentlessly. Would that justify oppression? That seems dubious. The difficulty with the Supreme Court's arguments for student rights is not unlike the difficulty with Mill's general arguments for liberty. They are consequentialist arguments. We need to appreciate the fact that when we justify our rights by appeals to dubious empirical claims we endanger them. Students, like other persons, are moral agents. That is why they have civil rights. When students are immature they may reasonably be subjected to some forms of paternalism concerning such rights when the point is to prevent unnecessary harm or to increase the maturity and autonomy of their judgement. Nevertheless, students are persons and deserve the respect appropriate to persons. The US Supreme Court seems to me to be correct in declaring students to be persons before the law. The Court, however, is wrong insofar as it seems to rule out any possibility of legitimate paternalism toward immature students in the exercise of their rights. Moreover, the Court errs both in appearing to extend the model of the marketplace of ideas uncritically to the teaching of disciplines and by relying too heavily on educational consequences to justify student rights.

This has been a long and complex argument. It requires a summary. The central point to affirm is that students do have rights. They are persons and moral agents, and must, therefore, be treated as objects of value and respect.

I have, however, argued several points that suggest that the rights of students in schools are not simply the civil rights of adults in society. Civil liberties are rooted in a presumption of equality between the parties, and their central point is to promote respect for persons and moral autonomy. In the classroom, the expert and the novice as citizens are equal, but they are not equally competent in academic subject matter. Moreover, the point of the classroom is that the student should come to internalize the concepts of the expert. It is not a marketplace of ideas where truth emerges from a multitude of tongues. It is a place where the student strives to master a rational enterprise under the guidance of an expert. Treating the expert–novice relationship as though it were governed by civil rights distorts its character.

I have also argued that paternalism is legitimate. Those who are not in the maturity of their faculties may be subjected to restrictions that would violate the rights of adults. The end of paternalism, however, must be to protect the immature from harm and to enhance their capacity for independent choice. Paternalism may occasionally be appropriate even with respect to rights such as free speech and press. This is not, however, permissibly used as a justification of censorship.

The most important observation to make is that the need to talk about student rights bespeaks the ill-health of education. It signifies either that students are alienated from adult values or that adults are abusing their trust. Education, more than most human institutions, requires trust. Litigation and formal regulations are foreign to its nature. That our educational systems have needed to attend to such matters may indicate a concern for fairness, but it also signifies the widespread failure to establish an environment in which adults and children, experts and novices, can interact with mutual respect and confidence. Perhaps the restoration of such trust and confidence should be our highest concern.

# The Nature of Nurture
# and the Role of the State

At the outset of this volume, I warned the reader that I was going to be primarily interested in the epistemology of liberty. As I wrote the words, my mind's ear heard vague mutterings from imagined readers. The mutterings expressed misgivings about the approach. 'What has the theory of knowledge got to do with freedom in education?' they asked. 'We would have thought that the question of freedom in learning had primarily to do with the motivation to learn and is really a question for psychologists, rather than philosophers.'

I hope the reader is by now persuaded that epistemology does have something to say about liberty and learning. On the other hand, the reader may also harbour the suspicion that I have left a considerable part of the topic untouched. What about questions of interest and motivation? Isn't there a story to tell here?

If I were to ask one of my undergraduate classes to give an argument for freedom in education, I would wager that a notable majority would provide a variant of the following: people learn best when they are learning what they are interested in. If they are to be interested in something, it must be related to their basic wants or needs. Moreover, if what students are learning is to be of interest to them, students must be able to decide what they will learn. Otherwise, there is no guarantee that what they learn will spring from their wants and needs or that they will be interested in it. Freedom is thus a handmaid to interest. Its point is to allow the learner to pursue his natural inclinations in learning.

This argument seems enormously appealing. Like most
150

appealing arguments, it has a grain of truth. I also believe it is largely wrongheaded. In some of its manifestations the argument has two basic assumptions. The first is a commitment to a kind of nativism. People are supposed to come into the world with native interests, talents and capacities. Perhaps these can be added to or expanded on, but they are there from the start. Interests, needs or wants are biological, rather than social phenomena. Carl Rogers, an American psychologist who has written extensively on the topic of freedom in education, illustrates this point nicely. In one article, he suggests that the infant is the paradigm of a free person because, not having been socialized, the infant is in touch with its real self and its real needs. Rogers writes,

> Another aspect of the infant's approach to value is that the source or locus of the evaluating process is clearly within himself. Unlike many of us he knows what he likes and dislikes, and the origin of those value choices lies strictly within himself. He is the center of the valuing process . . .[1]

Many modern advocacies of the nativist claim are a mixture of Rousseau with Freud. Education aims to develop or reveal natural capacities. It should be directed by the learner's inner inclinations. It must be natural. The enemy to natural education is repression. In the hands of some authors, such as Rogers, repression is virtually synonymous with socialization.

For Rogers, infants are the paradigm of autonomous choice because they have not yet encountered others who will tell them what they should like and who will lead them astray from their true self to some false self. Rogers seems to see the person as consisting of a real self overlayed with a social self. Genuine education involves the liberation of the real self.

These views are nativism with a vengeance. They view teaching (rather than facilitating learning) as somewhere between misguided and sinful. Teaching, after all, imposes ideas and values. Ideas and values that are taught do not arise from the inner self. Genuine learning permits the teacher only to supply resources that are required by the student's natural inclinations. The teacher can follow, but not lead.

It is an easy transition from this sort of nativism to the second assumption of the argument. If people have such natural inclinations that should be given free reign in their education, then they have a right not to be interfered with in the matter of being themselves. We thus have the potential of a view of rights developed primarily on the assumption that it is wrong to interfere with the natural growth of the individual. Liberty is the removal of constraint and the elimination of repression. People should become themselves, not what their society or their culture wishes them to be.

The best expression of this set of ideas I have encountered is in A. S. Neill's *Summerhill*:

> . . . we set out to make a school in which we should allow children freedom to be themselves. In order to do this, we had to renounce all discipline, all direction, all suggestion, all moral training, all religious instruction . . . All it required was what we had – a belief in the child as a good, not an evil, being.
>
> My view is that a child is innately wise and realistic. If left to himself without adult suggestion of any kind, he will develop as far as he is capable of developing.[2]

Neill's views seem to me to express in grand style the assumptions implicit in the argument with which we began. Human nature is good. People have a right to follow their inclinations in their education. The view is kind, optimistic and seductive. It is also wrong. It will, I believe, help to sharpen the views I have developed in earlier chapters to note its problems.

The basic deficiency is the strong strain of nativism. It is not clear exactly what is supposed to be innate. While Neill suggests that children are innately wise, it would be surprising to find that he believed that children had an innate knowledge of calculus or astronomy. And while he suggests that they are innately good, it would be surprising to find that he believed that children came into the world with a firm grasp on philosophical theories of justice. On the other hand, the tendency toward wisdom and goodness must be both significant and have some distinct content. To see why, we need to consider the role these innate tendencies have in Neill's thought. Firstly, his belief in these tendencies allows him to give some meaning to the idea of being one's self. Each individual apparently comes into the world with a real self, a personality structure, a set of preferences or inclinations that have enough focus to allow claims that in acting in some way people are, or are not, being themselves. This does not require that people be born with an innate desire to hear Beethoven's Fifth, for example, but it does perhaps require that a preference for classical music be rooted somehow in one's innate make-up. The second role this belief in an innate self performs is to establish a right not to be interfered with in pursuing one's basic inclinations. That is presumably related to its inherent goodness. The third role played by this real self is to allow Neill to dispense with the need for human and social resources in the child's development. That the child is innately good and innately wise means that social institutions that are intended to promote goodness and competence are unnecessary. Indeed, they are illegitimate in that they interfere with the child's natural growth.

It is particularly this last conclusion that I find problematic. It is educationally destructive in that it denies to children social resources on which their growth depends, except those that they see themselves to have need of. To put the point in a more fundamental way, it fails to see that becoming fully human depends on internalizing available social and cultural resources, not on some mysterious process of natural growth, and it fails to see that children are in no position to judge the value of these cultural social resources.

Neill seems most concerned with what might be called moral resources – discipline, direction, suggestion, moral training and religion. It is apparently illegitimate to suggest to a child that people have found some things and not others to be worthwhile, and have found that some ways of dealing with each other are moral, while others are not.

But consider an analogous claim. Let us suppose that someone regarding children as naturally wise and good was to argue that we ought not to teach a child a language until he had indicated which language (if any) he wanted to learn. Why, after all, should we impose English on a child whose native inclination might run towards French, Hebrew or Chinese? The absurdity of the suggestion is obvious. How is the child to choose? Having learned a language, the child may decide to learn another, or even to speak or modify his own in certain ways. But how would the child pick among human languages at the outset?

How do moral concepts differ? The answer is that they do not. Those who have been initiated into some set of values and moral ideas can adopt others or modify the ones they have. Having acquired a moral or valuational point of view, they have also acquired a tool that can be turned on itself. That is the nature of ideas. Lacking such concepts, no choice is possible. To suggest that children not receive moral training is not to leave them to a natural path of growth. Instead, the result will be that moral concepts will be acquired from haphazard and perhaps undesirable sources – television or peers. To succeed in withholding moral instruction from a child is to make that child amoral and pathological, and denies the child his right to become a moral agent.

This argument is, of course, simply the argument of the first part of the book applied to moral concepts. It is, however, more revealing of the basic commitment of my view. In essence, I am arguing that reality for human beings is social. People become human beings by learning from other human beings concepts, ideas, rules and procedures, which create for them the world in which they live. I have argued this theme with respect to intellectual disciplines, but that part of the argument is by no means unique to science. Concepts create a world. Without the rules of football, there is not an activity called scoring a goal; there is only kicking a ball into a net. Likewise in the moral area, without concepts there are no acts of kindness or unkindness, fairness or unfairness, or decency or indecency. To use Wittgenstein's felicitous phrase, becoming human, living in a public human world, is a matter of learning a set of forms of life, ways of seeing and interpreting the world.

It does not follow from this argument that all forms of life are equally valuable. Some may be better than others; some may be perverse. Such ways of seeing the world can be thought about, modified, improved or rejected in favour of better ones. But, like scientific ideas, they are not only the objects of thought, but the means.

If the human world is social in this way, the kind of nativism involved in Rogers and Neill, and implicit in the intuitive argument with which I began, has a number of severe defects. Most important, if taken seriously, it threatens to deny to children the resources on which their growth depends. Particularly in moral or valuational areas, the view virtually identifies socialization with oppression. The right values are those that come from within. It thus becomes anathema to impose values on the child – and impose here means little more than to try in any way to get the child to adopt the value. Any form of moral direction is offensive. Moreover, instruction in any area can be seen as offensive unless and until the child requests it. Education itself easily becomes seen as a morally dubious affair.

It is difficult, fortunately, for people to act consistently on such a view. Children exist in a social environment. It is about as likely that they can avoid socializing influences as it is that they can avoid getting wet while swimming. It is possible, however, to avoid deliberate, planned and systematic guidance and teaching for fear of imposing on the child's natural inclinations and directions.

We need not suppose that in order to teach children we must run roughshod over their values and inclinations. But values and inclinations themselves are substantially social products. Children learn what is worthwhile from other people. One need only observe children watching television to see the extent that wants are created, rather than appealed to, by advertising. Values are, for the most part, imbedded in the forms of life into which children are initiated. It is the point of education to initiate children into forms of life whose values promise to allow them to experience the world in satisfying and meaningful ways. There is, of course, something to be said for the notion that what people ultimately find satisfying and meaningful depends to an extent on human nature, or on the individual's nature. But if we see the contribution of nature as expressed in a highly focused set of values and preferences, rather than in broad directions that will be fulfilled and refined by learning, we will treat the child's initial direction and preferences as sacrosanct and will tend to withhold from them the cultural resources that can deepen and enhance their lives.

It may be urged that despite these sharp differences, the views I have argued have much in common with the views I am now criticizing. I have claimed rather often that my central moral commitments include moral agency and moral autonomy: people have a duty to be responsible for their judgements. Is this not what Neill and Rogers are arguing, too? Are they not interested in creating people who are independent and who are responsible for their own conduct?

I believe, in fact, they are not, or, if they are, they conceive this kind of moral independence quite differently from the way in which I view it. The point is best put in terms of a distinction between autonomy and authenticity. Autonomy is the capacity to make and act on independent reasoned judgements. It requires a grasp of the kind of intellectual skills and concepts appropriate to the choice at issue, and it requires the psychological capacities to allow reasons to be the source of choice and action. Autonomy is very much an achievement. It requires understanding and self-control. It is a quality that infants, who respond almost mechanically to internal and external stimuli, lack. Authenticity, by contrast, is a matter of choosing or acting consistently with one's nature, of being one's self, not being phony. It requires the ability to identify and act on one's genuine tastes and preferences.

Autonomy and authenticity are thus distinct. Both are worthwhile. Autonomy, however, is a fundamental value. It is a requirement of being a moral agent and being responsible for one's self and one's conduct. Authenticity is not similarly fundamental.

Here, however, I am concerned to note that authenticity is an easily perverted value. When the concept is linked to the notion that being one's self is a matter of acting on natural, rather than acquired, inclinations or preferences, it will lead people unreasonably to deny to children cultural sources of value. When children learn that they are entitled to authenticity, it can lead to narcissism and to an unwillingness to modify the pursuit of one's desires in consideration of the claims of others. A society that promotes authenticity may have cause to lament the reluctance with which its members give one another justice.

These remarks can be summarized by suggesting that *there is much to be said for the notion that persons – moral agents – are made, not born. Persons are significantly the result of initiating children into cultural resources for understanding, appreciating and acting. To the extent that the romantic tradition in education fails to understand this and seeks to substitute a 'natural education' for initiation into available cultural resources, it is perverse.*

The quality of the cultural and intellectual resources into which we seek to initiate people and the way we seek to do this are, of course, a matter of great concern. I do not propose to say any more on what is to count as a quality resource than what is implicit in what I have already said. But I do wish to address a still unresolved issue concerning who is entitled to decide about the education of children. First, I shall need to assemble some of the pieces of the issue from various sections of this book.

In the chapter on student rights I constructed an argument in defence of paternalism, but I left the question of who was entitled to exercise paternal authority open. That is the question to be addressed. I shall assume that the major options are the child's parents or the state. But it is not a question of choosing between parents and the state. It is a question of apportioning rights and responsibilities. What kinds of decisions are parents entitled to make about their children? What decisions can the state make? When can the state overrule parents or interfere in the family? In particular, when can the school act independently of or against the wishes of parents, and when must it accede to parental demands?

I shall discuss these issues employing some assumptions. I assume that in a free society governments are not normally entitled to act paternalistically toward their citizens. It is not sufficient justification for a government to interfere in a person's life that it believes it is acting in his interests. In a free society people are entitled to be the judge of their own interests. That is one implication of the value of moral agency. I also assume that governments are entitled to interfere in a person's life in order to promote the public interest. Governments may not use coercion to compel a person to act for his own good, but they may compel a person to act for the good of all.

But children are legitimately subjected to paternalism. Are they legitimately subjected to governmental paternalism against the consent of their parents? I shall argue the following theses. First, I shall claim that there is *prima facie* case in favour of the view that it is paents, not the state, who are entitled to paternal authority over children. This authority includes the right to control the child's education. Second, I shall claim that the state may override parental claims under two kinds of conditions: either when the assumptions that establish the *prima facie* case in favour of parental authority are rebutted, or when the public interest is at stake.

Consider first what can be said in favour of the right of parents to exercise paternal authority. There are three arguments. First, parents love their children. They are thus predisposed to act for the sake of the needs and interests of their children, sometimes to the point of self-sacrifice. Persons paid by the state to teach children may care for children but are less strongly disposed than parents to act for their interests. Second, parents know their children's interests. Parents are intimately acquainted with their children and are in a better position to understand their interests than are those who are paid by the state to teach or care for them. Third, parents have a stake in their children. The first two points assume that the central issue in deciding who is to be responsible for children is to determine what is in the best interest of the child. But parents are bound to the child by strong bonds of concern and affection. They may project their hopes and aspirations onto their children. They may experience the child's injuries, the child's successes, the child's failures as their own. These facts give parents a stake in their children. Moreover, many parents feel a strong moral duty to care for their children and a strong sense of responsibility for the well-being of their children. To interfere with the exercise of this responsibility, or to harm the child, is to harm the parent.

These claims establish a *prima facie* right of parents to determine the education and upbringing of their children. These claims are not, however, uniformly true. They should, therefore, be treated as rebuttable assumptions. Moreover, the state should be entitled to assume the normal role of parents when these assumptions are rebutted. I assume a strong assumption in favour of parent rights, but it is an assumption that can be overruled when parents treat their children malevolently or behave toward them in grossly incompetent ways.

The next question for us, however, is the nature of the public interest and when the public interest can override the rights of parents. We need to focus on the public's interest in education.

The idea of the public's interest in education concerns those cases where the consequences of learning – the benefits and the failures in education – affect people other than the particular individual who learns, or fails to learn. When a child learns, others may benefit. When a child fails, others may be harmed. I suggest the following as the major components of the public interest in education:

(1) *Neighbourhood effects:* the education of a given child can benefit not just the child but the entire society. Those educational benefits that accrue to persons other than the direct recipients of education are legitimate objects of public concern. Everyone benefits when an individual becomes economically productive or becomes a good citizen.

(2) *Prevention of incompetence:* some forms of incompetence, particularly political and economic incompetence, harm persons other than the individuals who are incompetent. The prevention of these kinds of incompetence is a legitimate public concern.

(3) *The promotion of justice:* this includes promoting equal opportunity, promoting a concern for and a sense of the meaning of justice, and promoting the abilities that permit people to function properly in a just society.

(4) *Promoting common forms of understanding:* while a stable society does not preclude pluralism, it does depend on individuals sharing enough of a common view of the world that they can interact harmoniously and communicate intelligibly.

These categories obviously overlap. They do, however, give a picture of the character of the public interest in education. Basic skills seem required by all of these components. Instruction in the ideals and practices of a free society serve the third point. A reasonable grasp of history, geography, mathematics, science and language serves several of the above, particularly the fourth point. These are the things in which the public interest in education is most clearly expressed.

When someone's unwillingness to learn poses a significant threat to the public interest, the state may be entitled to use coercion to protect its interests. Generally, when the public interest is at stake, the state is entitled to some form of control over education. This is the justification for compulsory education, for public financing of schooling, and for public regulation of privately financed or administered education. It is also the justification for governmental involvement in higher education.

Perhaps the central point to make here, however, is that the fact that the public has legitimate interests in education that entitle government to some forms of compulsion does not entail that government has a right to control everything about schooling. Schools normally provide educational resources and services that exceed the public's interest in education. They provide instruction in areas such as art, music or sports, which may be justified by individual need or demand, but which is not required by the public interest. And they provide instruction in areas that are required by the public interest to a degree that exceeds the demands of the public interest. The public has a considerable interest in widespread literacy. It is doubtful if it has such an interest in a widespread knowledge of Shakespeare. Moreover, particularly in dealing with younger children, schools often concern themselves with the students' lives and conduct in ways that exceed the public interest. They may interest themselves deeply in the child's moral and social development. Indeed, much emphasis is given to the idea of educating the whole child. Little attention is paid to the question of how much of the whole child is the legitimate concern of the state.

My point here is not to argue that when a school is funded or administered by a government agency it should limit itself to those kinds of education that are clearly related to the public interest and leave other kinds of education to private agencies. There may be occasions when that is sensible, but normally it is not. To separate the public and private components of education in this way is surely inefficient. Moreover, it assumes that the public/private distinction is a sharp conceptual tool capable of generating a clear distinction between different components of education. Unfortunately, it is at best a rather blunt instrument.

The point is instead to insist that it is inappropriate for the state to use the fact that it supports or administers schools that serve the public interest in order to extend its authority over the private components of education. This point is particularly important concerning how we are to think of the authority schools exercise over young children and the relations between the school and the child's parents. The school may sometimes exercise authority over a child because it is pursuing the public interest. In such cases it may overrule the wishes of the child's parents. If a child's parents wish not to have their child taught to read, the school is within its rights to teach him to read in any case. In the private sphere, however, the school has no inherent right to control the child or his education. There is a presumption that the child's parents are entitled to control his education. Unless this presumption has been refuted, or the state has shown some state interest overriding this presumption, the parent's rights continue in force.

This leads to the conclusion that any authority that schools exercise over children beyond those areas that significantly affect the state's interests must be seen as delegated authority. The schools quite literally stand in the place of parents and exercise the authority of parents. I do not believe this requires the school to obtain parental permission for every act it takes. I do, however, believe that it requires schools to exhibit a high level of concern for parental views. Moreover, it indicates that schools have a burden of proof to bear whenever they act contrary to the expressed wishes of a child's parents. They may meet this burden of proof either by rebutting the presumption that the parents are acting for the sake of the child, or by showing that the public interest is involved in some significant way. Otherwise, they are obliged to acquiesce to the parent's desires. Children are not the property of the state so that state-operated schools are entitled to comprehensive control of their education.

I would like to test this framework by posing a hard case. The United States is currently undergoing a kind of conservative revival. One of the most conspicuous manifestations of this is some pressure on schools to be more responsive to the views of conservative parents, especially those parents with conservative religious views. Among the issues that have been raised are these: there have been numerous attempts to have books removed from school libraries or reading lists for English classes. Such books are commonly regarded as obscene, religiously offensive or un-American. Nothing very clear is conveyed by the label 'un-American', although it is normally applied to books that are critical of some American policy or that express leftist views. There have also been numerous objections to various course offerings that touch on morally sensitive issues. Sex education and moral education are frequent targets. Recently there has been much public agitation concerning the teaching of evolution. The normal basis for objecting to such courses is that they are seen as conflicting with the beliefs or values of traditional religion.

How are we to think about these issues? School officials have often resisted removing books or dropping courses. They have defended their actions by appealing to the concept of academic freedom and by holding that offended parents may have a right to prevent their own children from being exposed to ideas that they perceive as offensive, but they do not have a right to impose their views on others. They have also often excused the children of protesting parents from the offending courses and denied them access to the offending books. Presumably they would argue that parents have the right to choose for their children in such areas. Some American courts have held that parents, in fact, have a right to withdraw their children from offending courses unless the school can demonstrate a compelling public interest in compulsory attendance at these courses.

The line of argument I have developed in this chapter would seem to support this result. Parents should retain control over the education of their children in such areas. Nevertheless, a plausible case can be made that the values I have defended throughout this book make a strong case against the view that parents should be entitled to withdraw their children from such courses or to deny them access to books they find offensive. I have generally argued that liberty serves the values of rationality and moral agency, and that people have a right to the resources that allow them to develop their potential for autonomous choice and to the information necessary for competent and responsible choices. Here, however, I have accepted a policy that allows parents to withhold such resources from their own children. Do censorship and indoctrination become more acceptable when parents do it to their own children?

The first question to ask is whether in such cases the school can justify overriding the parents' wishes by appealing to the criteria already developed. Can it rebut the presumption of the parents' right to control the education of their children, or can it show some important state interest is at stake?

To rebut the presumption of parental control, the school might argue three different claims: that such parents are not acting for the sake of the well-being of their children, that they lack an understanding of the genuine interests of their children, or that they have no stake in the education of their children. The first and third arguments are not plausible. Parents who protest at the curriculum the school seeks to provide for their children by the very act exhibit concern for their children and suggest that they have a stake in the education of their children. The second argument, however, has considerable plausibility. Parents who resist the school when it appears to act in ways that violate their religious convictions and their attempt to transmit them to their children may act out of love for their children and may have a stake in the education of their children, but they may lack a reasonable view of the interests of their children. I have argued that all children have an interest in moral agency and autonomous choice. These are not just interests, but quite fundamental ones. Arguably, parents who fail to pursue these interests for their children are denying them fundamental rights. Here, then, is a line of argument that might be used to rebut the presumption that parents meet the minimal requirements for maintaining control over the upbringing of their children.

There is also an argument that suggests that the state has a significant interest in the moral agency and autonomy of children. These traits are properly seen as components of citizenship. They are presupposed by the institutions of a free society. Moral agency and autonomy are the values that liberty serves. Moreover, a free society requires people to take responsibility for their own lives if it is to remain a free society. Plausible arguments can, therefore, be given to suggest that schools are entitled to overrule parental control over the education of their children when parents act so as to censor what their children read, or to restrict the ideas with which they come in contact. When the school acts against the will of the parents in such cases, it is acting for the sake of a fundamental interest of the child and for the sake of an important public interest. These interests are sufficiently important to override the rights of parents.

I find these arguments to be powerful, but not finally persuasive. There are other arguments that I believe support parents' rights in such matters.

The first argument concerns the lack of clarity of the issues in conjunction with the fact that religious beliefs or fundamental convictions are involved. It is one thing to describe in philosophical terms when schools might be entitled to overrule parental wishes. It is quite another to translate such concerns into a workable and enforceable standard. After all, parents who object to some component of the curriculum are unlikely to see themselves as restricting their child's growth. They are far more likely to believe that they are preventing the child from encountering ideas that are morally or intellectually corrupting. How clear is it that the school and not the parents is right? Could we establish any general criteria for such a judgement independently of particular facts? Most importantly, could we make a judgement on such issues without making a judgement on the merits of some set of religious doctrines?

Consider a contrast between this kind of case and an analogous case. A religious sect, called Jehovah's Witnesses, has beliefs that preclude blood transfusions. Several cases have arisen in the United States in which Jehovah's Witnesses have refused permission for a blood transfusion for one of their children under conditions where the child's life was at stake. Courts have sometimes intervened in such cases, granting the transfusions over the objections of parents. This case differs from the educational cases in that it is clear that a fundamental interest of the child – his life – is at stake. The interest is basic. It is hard to imagine one more basic. Medical knowledge also allows a reasonable degree of certainty in such matters. We can be sure that the action of the parents is, in fact, threatening the life of the child.

The religious convictions of the parents are, of course, also threatened. Indeed, it is clearer in this case than in the educational cases that the decision to overrule the parents' wishes is rooted in the presumption that their religious preferences are wrong. It may be, however, that the threat to the parents' religious convictions is less severe in this case than in the educational cases, for here no attempt need be made to influence the religious beliefs of parent or child. The parents are, rather, precluded from acting on their convictions in a single, narrowly defined case. In the educational cases, the ability of parents successfully to transmit their religious convictions to their children is at stake.

The central point here is that the educational cases involve a potential clash between the state and the individual's religious convictions under circumstances where it is difficult to imagine how coherent enforceable rules could be developed and where the potential conflict between public power and religious liberty is profound. It seems unwise to give the state power over an issue where religious interests are concerned when it is difficult to describe rules and procedures that clearly delineate and confine the use of that power.

It is important to recognize that there is a substantial threat involved to the freedom of conscience of parents in any educational venture that has the potential to prevent parents from transmitting their religious convictions to their children. Religious convictions are fundamental convictions. They serve to define the meaning of life and existence. To cause a person to disavow or act contrary to his religious convictions is an act of great violence against that person. Moreover, religions characteristically assign to parents the duty to raise their children in the faith. To prevent a parent from fulfilling this duty can likewise be an act of violence against the parent. Perhaps there are cases in which the interests of the child or the state demand such intervention. Such cases should be both clear and compelling. In these cases there are important interests of the child at stake. They are not, however, so clearly or compellingly at stake as to justify the intervention of the state into the religious life of the family.

There is one more line of argument on this issue I wish to explore. It is an epistemological argument. In chapter 4 I discussed the marketplace of ideas as a defence of the civil right of free expression. I took a dim view of that argument, primarily on the grounds that the marketplace of ideas had no way to judge ideas rationally. That function was best served by intellectual communities. Here I want to reconsider that argument and to modify it modestly.

In the argument on academic freedom, I suggested that norms of intellectual tolerance could be applied in two contexts. One had to do with the generation of ideas, the second with their selection. A society that wishes to be intellectually progressive must have both sources of intellectual novelty and ways to refine and select among the novelties generated.

Ideas are often generated within intelletual communities. Unsolved problems and anomalous phenomena are often the stimulus for new ideas. Intellectual communities are in a unique position to be aware of such things. We should not, however, lose sight of the extent to which novelties that are ultimately incorporated into the views of members of intellectual communities occur outside those communities. The great dangers of intellectual communities are conservatism and irrelevance. Such communities can continue to enforce their intellectual traditions beyond reason and to the point where they cease to speak to the contemporary world. They thus need external sources of novelty for their renewal. Those who know the history of philosophy will, I hope, be sensitive to the extent to which individuals, ideas and events that have changed the field have come from outside.

Thus, the arguments made about tolerance in the context of academic freedom apply also to the broader domain of the social marketplace of ideas. The arguments of chapter 4 make a reasonable case that the social marketplace of ideas cannot be expected to perform the task of intellectual selection since society lacks shared intellectual standards by which ideas can be assessed. This function is best accomplished within communities with shared standards. The social marketplace of ideas cannot effectively judge and reject ideas because it is too tolerant. But it is an important source of novelty. It is good at producing ideas, practices and experiences to think about. Here a high level of tolerance is a substantial virtue. A lack of tolerance will reduce cultural variety and in doing so will narrow the cultural resources for producing those novelties on which the renewal of human thought and affairs depends.

An analogous argument can be constructed concerning the context of individual choice. Individuals seeking to take responsibility for the direction of their lives need a rich and varied set of options from which to choose. They, too, require a society capable of generating novelties. Thus, a rich and diverse culture with ample opportunity for novelties to occur is a resource both for the life of intellectual communities and for individuals seeking to make responsible and rational choices. Tolerance for cultural novelty is, thus, a considerable virtue.

The point of this argument so far as schooling is concerned is that the school can easily become a device whereby cultural diversity and novelty are reduced. Schools operate in the direction of producing cultural and intellectual uniformity. I do not mean to suggest by this that they behave illegitimately or coercively. However, the curriculum of the schools is, to a significant extent, under the influence of the members of intellectual communities. The centre of the curriculum of most schools is academic disciplines – mathematics, science and language. The context of instruction is influenced strongly by those who write the texts and teach the courses. These people either are members of intellectual communities, or are dependent on them for what they teach.

In initiating children into these enterprises, the school also exerts influence by means of which at least some components of the cultural heritage are refereed by intellectual communities. I do not object to this process. Indeed, I quite approve since it serves to acquaint children with intellectual resources of proven worth, and since some commonalities in a society's cultural heritage are essential to its stability. But the process shares in the weakness of intellectual communities. At their worst, they can be conservative and inadequately open to novelty. It thus seems important that schools do not operate in such a way that they gratuitously suppress novelty. But we do just this when we compel students from traditions at odds with some component of the curriculum to attend to it, nonetheless. We should, I think, be confident enough in the intellectual heritage represented in the school curriculum to teach it without apology. We should not be so confident in it to assume that sources of novelty outside of these traditions are unnecessary. This seems to me to be an additional reason to support parents who wish not to have their children taught something at odds with parental beliefs. To support such parents is to support diversity, and to provide a society with sources of renewal.

This postscript has been intended to deal with some odds and ends of issues that were generated in the central thread of the argument but not attended to there. Its results are as follows:

(1) Views of freedom in education that seek to 'liberate' children from the intellectual heritage taught by most schools are to be resisted. They neglect the extent to which genuine liberation depends on intellectual competence and the extent to which the resources for intellectual competence reside in some intellectual heritage.

(2) Parents and the state have a stake in what goes on in education. Schools must respect the rights of parents over the education of their children and the legitimate authority of the state to make decisions concerning public matters.

(3) The values of rationality, moral agency and autonomy are the central values to be considered in a theory of freedom in education. Nevertheless, they are not the only human values and may sometimes need to be balanced against other values such as the sanctity of the family and religious duties and convictions.

I conclude simply by reminding the reader of the main theme of this volume. A cogent view of liberty and learning needs to have a coherent view of the role of received ideas. Common notions of liberty were formed when received ideas had too much authority. But we cannot lose sight of the fact that received ideas are also intellectual tools. As such they must have at least provisional authority. The precise nature of this authority is the centre issue of liberty and learning.

# Notes

*Chapter 1*
1. Quoted from Carl R. Rogers, *Freedom to Learn*. Columbus, Ohio: Charles E. Merrill, 1969, p. i'.
2. John Stuart Mill, *On Liberty*. New York: Bobbs Merrill Co., 1956, pp. 71–2.
3. *Sweezy v. New Hampshire*, 354 U.S. 234.
4. Milton Friedman, *Capitalism and Freedom*. Chicago: University of Chicago Press, 1962, pp. 85–6.
5. *ibid.*, p. 86.

*Chapter 2*
1. Stephen Toulmin, *Human Understanding*. Princeton: Princeton University Press, 1972, p. 35.
2. Peter Medawar, *Induction and Intuition in Scientific Thought*. Philadelphia: American Philosophical Society, 1969, p. 11.
3. Thomas S. Kuhn, *The Structure of Scientific Revolutions*. Chicago: University of Chicago Press, 1962.

*Chapter 4*
1. Mill, *On Liberty, op. cit.,* p. 14.
2. *ibid.,* p. 13.
3. *ibid.,* p. 64.
4. *ibid.,* p. 81.
5. John Stuart Mill, *Utilitarianism*, reprinted in *The Utilitarians*. New York: Doubleday and Company, 1961, p. 410.

*Chapter 5*
1. Douglas Peterson, 'The American cause and the American university', reprinted in Immanuel Wallerstein and Paul Star, *The*

*University Crisis Reader.* New York: Random House, 1971, Vol. 1, pp. 72–3.

2. Robert Paul Wolff, *The Ideal of the University.* Boston: Beacon Press, 1969, pp. 70–1.

*Chapter 6*

1. *Tinker v. Des Moines*, 393 U.S. 509.
2. *ibid.,* p. 512.
3. Mill, *On Liberty*, *op. cit.,* p. 13.
4. *ibid.,* p. 14.
5. *ibid.,* p. 71.
6. James Coleman *et al., Youth: Transition to Adulthood.* Chicago: Chicago University Press, 1974, p. 124.

*Postscript*

1. Rogers, *Freedom to Learn, op. cit.,* p. 243.
2. A. S. Neill, *Summerhill.* New York: Hart Publishing Company, 1960, p. 4.

# Further Reading

The following works are intended to assist the student who wishes to do further work on the topics I have discussed in this book. They are arranged by topic rather than by chapter, since it seems to me that this sort of arrangement would provide a more useful classification. I have not attempted to be comprehensive in this list. Rather, I have simply mentioned things I have read from which I have profited.

## GENERAL BOOKS ON FREEDOM

Bay, Christian, *The Structure of Freedom* Stanford, California: Stanford University Press, 1970.

Berlin, Isaiah *Four Essays on Liberty* London: Oxford University Press, 1969.

Fromm, Eric *Escape from Freedom* New York: Holt, Rinehart & Winston, 1965.

Hampshire, Stuart *Freedom of the Individual* New York: Harper and Row, 1965.

Hook, Sidney (Ed.) *Determinism and Freedom* New York: Collier Books, 1961.

## RIGHTS, LIBERTY, AND J. S. MILL

Benn, S. I., and Peters, R. S. *The Principles of Political Thought* New York: The Free Press, 1959.
*Social Principles and the Democratic State* London: Allen and Unwin, 1959.

Dworkin, Ronald *Taking Rights Seriously* Cambridge, Massachusetts: Harvard University Press, 1977.

Hayek, Friedrich *The Constitution of Liberty* Chicago: University of Chicago Press, 1960.

Himmelfarb, Gertrude *On Liberty and Liberalism: The Case of John Stuart Mill* New York: Alfred A. Knopf, 1974.

Hobhouse, L. T. *Liberalism* London: Oxford University Press, 1964.

Rawls, John *A Theory of Justice* Cambridge, Massachusetts: Harvard University Press, 1972.

Wolff, Robert Paul *The Poverty of Liberalism* Boston: Beacon Press, 1968.

Wolff, Robert Paul, Moore, Barrington, and Marcuse, Herbert *A Critique of Pure Tolerance* Boston: Beacon Press, 1965.

## PHILOSOPHY AND SOCIOLOGY OF SCIENCE

Elkana, Yehuda (Ed.) *The Interaction Between Science and Philosophy* Atlantic Highlands, New Jersey: Humanities Press, 1974.

Lakatos, Imre, and Musgrave, Alan (Eds.) *Criticism and the Growth of Knowledge* Cambridge, Massachusetts: Cambridge University Press, 1970.

Menton, Robert, *The Sociology of Science* Chicago: University of Chicago Press, 1974.

Toulmin, Stephen, *Human Understanding* Princeton, New Jersey: Princeton University Press, 1972.

## ACADEMIC FREEDOM

Hook, Sidney (Ed.) *In Defense of Academic Freedom* New York: Bobbs-Merrill, 1971.

Pincoffs, Edmund (Ed.) *The Concept of Academic Freedom* Austin, Texas: University of Texas Press, 1972.

Wolff, Robert Paul, *The Ideal of the University* Boston, Massachusetts: Beacon Press, 1969.

## STUDENT RIGHTS

Adams, Paul, *et al. Children's Rights* New York: Praeger Publishers, 1971.

Haubrich, Vernon F., and Apple, Michael *Schooling and the Rights of Children* Berkeley, California: McCutchan Publishing Corporation, 1975.

— Houlgate, Laurence D. *The Child and the State* Baltimore, Maryland:

The Johns Hopkins University Press, 1980.

Strike, Kenneth, and Egan, Kieran (Eds.) *Ethics and Educational Policy* London: Routledge and Kegan Paul, 1978.

Wringe, C. *Children's Rights: A Philosophical Study* London: Routledge and Kegan Paul, 1981.


## OPEN EDUCATION AND FREE SCHOOLS

Barrow, Robin *Radical Education: a Critique of Freeschooling and Deschooling* Oxford: Martin Robertson 1978.

Freire, Paulo *Pedagogy of the Oppressed* New York: Seabury Press, 1968.

Graubard, Allen *Free the Children* New York: Vintage Books, 1974.

Nyberg, David *The Philosophy of Open Education* London: Routledge and Kegan Paul, 1975.

Peters, R. S., and Dearden, R. F. (Eds.) *Perspectives on Plowden* London: Routledge and Kegan Paul, 1969.

# Index

175